This book belongs to: ~~Kathy Ramona Rodgers~~

Implementing PeopleSoft Financials

Implementing PeopleSoft Financials

A Guide for Success

EARLY STEPHENS

MANNING

Greenwich
(74° w. long.)

For electronic browsing of this book, see http://www.browsebooks.com

The publisher offers discounts on this book when ordered in quantity. For more information, please contact:

Special Sales Department
Manning Publications Co.
3 Lewis Street
Greenwich, CT 06830
Fax: (203) 661-9018
email: orders@manning.com

⊛ Recognizing the importance of preserving what has been written, it is Manning's policy to have the books it publishes printed on acid-free paper, and we exert our best efforts to that end.

Many of the designations used by manufacturers and sellers to distinguish their products are claimed as trademarks. Where those designations appear in the book, and Manning Publications was aware of a trademark claim, the designations have been printed in initial caps or all caps.

Library of Congress Cataloging-in-Publication Data
Stephens, Early
    Implementing PeopleSoft Financials / Early Stephens.
      p.   cm.
    Includes bibliographical references and index.
    ISBN 1-884777-35-X (pbk.)
    1. Management information systems.   2. PeopleSoft Financials.
I. Stephens, Early.
T58.6.I463 1996
657'.0285'53769—dc21   96-45699
                                            CIP

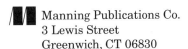 Manning Publications Co.
3 Lewis Street
Greenwich, CT 06830

Copyeditor: Katherine Antonsen
Typesetter: Nicholas A. Kosar
Cover designer: Leslie Haimes

Printed in the United States of America
7 8 9 10 – CR – 00 99

Dedicated to

Chris, Jan, Joe, and Tom—a true "A-Team"
and
Joanie, Lee, and Sam
for their patience and support

Thanks, Guys!

acknowledgments

The following individuals contributed to this book either directly or indirectly.

Thomas R. Wolf, Jr., Joseph Hulsebus, Christine Roberts, Teri Weese, Alan Orr, Jan Van Der Kley, Cameron Hair, Len Dorfman, Ted Kennedy, Marjan Bace, Christine Comaford, Robert Beam, Dale Jansen, Theresa Field

contents

preface

In the earliest years of my professional life I had the luxury of working closely with a somewhat autonomous group to develop software applications to support our nation's courts. My personal forte was child support and enforcement. For two years I worked in that role all the while learning as much about motivation, management, work style, team-work and success as I did about software development. That stint was followed by many years as a manager of software projects at a major university in my home town. During the first part of that I made myself a student of software development. I focused not so much on "what is the best way" to develop software. Instead, I studied the different tools and techniques available and their overall effectiveness. Then, due to the stress of managing multiple, large and important projects concurrently with a small staff, I began to shift my focus to a study of project management, or project *leadership* as I prefer to call it. I recognized that more often than not, projects were ending up less than successful.

This is about the time that visual development tools, object-oriented design and programming and client/server in general arrived on the scene. This complicated the problems developers and project teams faced. The technology was becoming more complex and more people were involved in the projects. The proliferation of local area networks and personal computers had created a class of demanding end-users—something we Information Systems professionals were not at all comfortable with. It was at this time that I saw an opportunity in these changes. I saw a chance to change my organization for the better by developing information systems applications a different way so as to provide greater productivity and better information to those who needed it wherever they might reside in the organization.

Also at this time, the university purchased PeopleSoft Human Resource Management System and followed that closely with the Financial applications. This convinced me further of the growing importance of information to an organization's success. During the implementations of PeopleSoft, I learned much about these issues as well as about the trials of the projects themselves. PeopleSoft brought great change to many organizations significantly for the better. It brought many improvements to the university as well. Politics and limited resources left me thirsting for significant growth instead of the incremental growth we had experienced. My frustration level increased as I saw more and more opportunity. The Internet was pushing its way beyond its academic walls and was poised to take the world by storm. To ease my frustrations, I moved on to greater challenges where I had an opportunity to apply my studies. To exercise my demons, though, I needed another outlet. That is where this book comes in. I so profoundly believe that this is a defining period for organizations world-wide that I feel compelled to help my fellow Americans in the corporate world succeed wildly because of it. This book represents my efforts to help them attain higher levels of success based on my experience with the software and years of studying information systems projects. To that end, writing it did provide me an outlet. To fully exercise those demons, though, this book must actually help corporations to have more successful implementations of PeopleSoft applications and to make them more competitive because of it. If it can do that for even one project team, then I feel my hard work will not have been in vain and the resistance to change I faced will be replaced with a sense of success and closure.

introduction

My first exposure to that exciting, new technology known as PeopleSoft was preceded by a flurry of emotions. I was excited by the opportunity to work with client/server technology. I was also very much aware of just how little I knew about it. Here was a new software suite, which brought with it such promise. We finally had the chance to make some real improvements for our end users and, at the same time, make enormous gains in the types of technologies and services we in the central information systems department could provide. It was one of those rare turning points in a career where, whether for better or for worse, I would never again be the same "professional." If things went right, this would change me, my department, and our end users for the better. If not, it carried the potential to ruin our careers and permanently affect our lives.

The software was, at that time, in its infancy. As such, precious little implementation help was even available. During the implementation of the first module, General Ledger, we learned many lessons. In fact, many decisions made in the interest of time and without all the requisite understanding were, in retrospect, incorrect. Some had to be "undone" over time, while others will remain intact because of the implications a change carries with it. Had the experience and understanding of a PeopleSoft Financials implementation been available when we needed it, our implementation would have been much smoother and our end users would have seen even more improvements. That brings me to this book. It is my sincere hope that by reading this book you can avoid some of the pitfalls facing you and your implementation team. I also hope to sow the seeds of a new way of thinking: starting a transformation from a traditional organization into one based on leadership and knowledgeable workers—a transformation that understands the magnitude and role of information in today's competitive industries.

Objective   The objective of this book is to help guide the reader to a successful PeopleSoft Financials implementation. It will draw upon the experiences and insights of others who have successfully implemented PeopleSoft Financials. It will present a finite list of issues to address, pitfalls to avoid, and opportunities to seize. It will school the unfamiliar in the technology that is PeopleSoft. It will endeavor to coax readers to formalize their approach so as to reach a timely, successful, and expected project end. Given the nature of client/server and software in general, it is impossible to present specifics for everyone to follow; however, the book will bring to light issues critical for a successful PeopleSoft Financials implementation. By drawing from this experience and insight, the reader will be armed and ready for success.

Intended audience   This book is targeted to everyone involved in a PS/Financials implementation. From the programmer trainee and the entry-level accounting clerk, through the senior implementation staff and management team, to the executive sponsors of the project: All will need to be informed and together have common expectations for a PeopleSoft Financials project to be successful. To that end, anyone involved in the implementation, after reading this book, will have a firm grasp on the issues at hand. Then, team dynamics will be free to succeed or fail on a level playing field.

How to read this book   You can read this book chapter by chapter, sequentially. This is the typical strategy. However, it is organized in such a way that chapters totally irrelevant to an individual may be skipped entirely—for example, the executive sponsor will likely not want to read the detailed workings of PeopleTools. He or she would probably skim that chapter to get flavor. A database administrator might want to pick and choose topics such as PeopleTools and Security in Chapter 2, which are relevant to his or her area of responsibility, and skim or skip the remainder of the book. The reader may also reread individual chapters to gain a better understanding of a specific topic.

chapter 1

PeopleSoft Financials

"There is nothing more difficult to plan, more doubtful of success, nor more dangerous to manage than the creation of a new system. For the initiator has the enmity of all who would profit by the preservation of the old system and merely lukewarm defenders in those who would gain by the new one."

—*Machiavelli, 1513*

PeopleSoft Financials is a complete, integrated, flexible suite of financial applications suitable for practically any corporate or public sector organization. It is, in every sense of the word, client/server software. The suite is comprised of a technology platform and common financial modules, such as general ledger, accounts receivable, and asset management. Included also is a robust, batch-processing environment complete with a program and job-scheduling system. It ships with a powerful financial reporting environment made up of standard, operational reports and a rich end-user reporting toolset. Flexibility and power are hallmarks of its reporting toolset. The software is scalable to fit organizations of any size: from the small, privately held corporation to the "Fortune 100." While the applications are both functional and flexible, it is often the technology platform, known collectively as PeopleTools, that catches the eyes of leading-edge corporations throughout the world. PeopleSoft is a unique company with a unique product line. As such, a close look at the critical success factors involved in a PeopleSoft Financials implementation is warranted.

1.1 The company

The concept of PeopleSoft, the company, originated from a corporate software visionary, Dave Duffield. In the mid-1980s, during his tenure as a senior manager at Integral Systems, Duffield began to visualize a new paradigm in corporate computing. He saw information attaining a new, strategic rank in organizations, and he saw workers becoming more and more dependent upon that information. He also knew that traditional, transaction-based software systems did precious little to fill this need. Executives at Integral were not receptive to Duffield's new ideas in software, so he teamed up with a technical guru and, in 1987, founded PeopleSoft in Walnut Creek, California. The company's initial, flagship product was PeopleSoft HRMS, a client/server human resource management and payroll system. Eight whirlwind years later, PeopleSoft is a corporate phenomenon with 1996 revenues of $200,000,000. Revenues have nearly doubled each year since 1988. In spite of the phenomenal growth, PeopleSoft retains most of the entrepreneurial characteristics that catapulted it to the spotlight.

PeopleSoft prides itself on being radically customer-focused, and it has taken steps to create an environment where this value can thrive. A visit to corporate headquarters will find the entire staff dressed in casual garb. It will also be conspicuously void of secretarial staff. PeopleSoft claims all employees, top to bottom, still write their own memos. PeopleSoft was chosen as one of "25 Cool Companies" by *Fortune Magazine* (July 10, 1995). And its approach reflects this coolness as a penchant for breaking corporate stereotypes in refreshing ways. "When the Gap came calling, the PeopleSoft sales team and members of top management wore Gap khakis."[*] That was a small gesture demonstrating PeopleSoft's

---

[*] *Fortune Magazine,* July 10, 1995

interest in its customers and its commitment to them and their success. In fact, Duffield buys stock in all of his customers' companies. It may be more accurate to say that an organization is a customer *with* PeopleSoft rather than *of* PeopleSoft. Unlike some software vendors, this relationship continues even after the contracts are signed.

According to my experience, the company listens zealously to its customers and addresses their concerns to further entrench their loyalty. In this way, PeopleSoft maintains an enthusiastic, committed, and positive advocacy group to help it sell to new clients. PeopleSoft justifies hefty profits by telling its customer base, "You really want your software company to continue growing." This appears to be a clever way to disguise what is really a serious liability for PeopleSoft: fast growth. Such growth brings with it a host of problems, and PeopleSoft has found no exemption from them.

The growth has not visibly affected the maturation of the software. It has, however, caused problems in customer service areas. PeopleSoft uses an "account manager" strategy to maintain the client relationships. The account manager position has been somewhat of a revolving door. As its customer base expanded and the company's organization grew in response, account managers were moved into management positions, moved into different product sectors, or transferred to different geographical regions. Some customers have seen as many as three different account managers within a single year. The account manager is the communication point between the customer and PeopleSoft and this "revolving door" position has clogged communication lines and negatively affected the implementations of some of its customers.

The demand for qualified, PeopleSoft-knowledgeable employees has created an employees' market. With head hunters actively seeking PeopleSoft experience and a consulting market that can fetch as high as $250 per hour, retaining the best talent continues to be a concern for PeopleSoft. The high growth rate has also created a rather diluted talent pool. It is not uncommon to hire a consultant, either from PeopleSoft or a third-party firm, pay $175 per hour, and be assigned a young developer with only two or three years of experience. With great care, however, organizations can find extremely talented and helpful professionals who can make a major contribution to their projects. The bottom line: Expect to pay for that talent. Organizations who are prone to sticker shock will find it in the PeopleSoft consulting market.

Another area where growth caused a noticeable problem is in hotline support. Duffield's tongue-in-cheek goal is to have a hotline support staff of zero. Ironically, at times it seemed that the hotline staff had that as a working goal. It can be a difficult and time-consuming process to solve a tricky, technical problem, because PeopleSoft's hotline staff may not assign someone with appropriate technical expertise. One organization struggled to get PeopleSoft's Process Scheduler, a batch-processing job scheduler, for eight months before a technician finally realized that the customer needed a special Windows NT version of the programming language, SQR. The lack of ORACLE on Windows NT experience at the hotline made this a major customer problem, when it might have been solved in the first two days.

The company appears to have reached critical mass in both hotline staff and account management staff. Since the release of PeopleSoft 5 in late 1995, the hotline support has been improving steadily, and the account management staff appears to have stabilized somewhat. PeopleSoft has reached a level where its customer service staff can develop specialized knowledge and skills while maintaining the breadth of coverage required by its customers. The rapid growth continues to be a problem for PeopleSoft and its clients, but less so as time passes.

One of PeopleSoft's most valuable assets is its lack of legacy baggage. Whereas most companies entered the client/server market with a large customer base, legacy products to support, and some entrenched paradigms about corporate software, PeopleSoft came to the table with a vision. They have built their products and customer base from the ground up. They have been able to bring products to market relatively quickly without the overhead a large customer base would entail.

The organization shares some characteristics with its software. PeopleSoft encourages and nurtures entrepreneurial work style. It pushes decision making into regional offices, closer to its customers, where they can be more closely aligned with the region's specific needs. Energy, enthusiasm, creativity, success, camaraderie, and customer focus: These characteristics typify the "PeopleSoft Personality." Probably because of Duffield's success in creating this corporate culture, the company has prospered in spite of the pressures of such growth. PeopleSoft has indeed thrived and brought a client/server suite of applications unlike any other to market.

1.2 The PeopleSoft Financials modules

PeopleSoft Financials is comprised of a group of separate but integrated modules all built around a powerful general ledger system. The modules can be mixed and matched in combination with one another. Organizations may purchase only those modules they need without being forced to implement all of them. (See Figure 1.1.)

1.2.1 General Ledger

PeopleSoft General Ledger is the foundation of their financials suite. Its capabilities include the ability to enter journals online or in batch and post them to the general ledger, open item and interunit accounting, allocations for flexible distribution of expenses, support for multiple currencies, average daily balance calculations, consolidations for combining the financial information of multiple operating entities, flexible year-end close processing, maintaining budgets, and robust financial reporting.

Some strengths of PeopleSoft General Ledger include the following:

- A flexible chart of accounts
- An unlimited number of ledgers

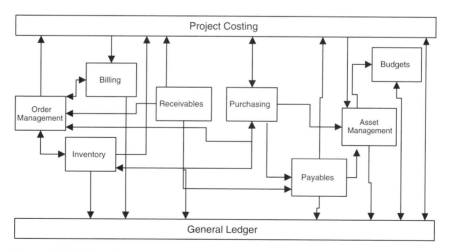

Figure 1.1 Relationship between PeopleSoft Financials modules

- Effective-date financial information
- Outstanding financial reporting tools including integration with Microsoft Excel
- Report summarization using PeopleSoft trees (see Section 2.5)

Its table-driven design and flexibility, coupled with the extensibility inherent in all PeopleSoft products, make PS/GL a viable option for most organizations. It is designed to take on the characteristics of an organization and then grow with it as business requirements change.

1.2.2 Accounts Payable

PeopleSoft Accounts Payable is a robust application which allows organizations to manage cash disbursements and related payables information. Its processes include maintaining vendor information, entering vouchers and scheduling them for payment, approving vouchers, matching vouchers (two-, three-, and four-way matching), defining and scheduling payments, forecasting payments, generating checks and EFT and reconciling the accounts, generating general ledger entries from payables data, and 1099 reporting.

A major strength of the application is its integration with PeopleSoft Purchasing for extensive voucher-matching options. It shares several tables with General Ledger, including chart field tables and calendars. The payables journal generation process can create journal entries directly in the General Ledger tables. It has a robust payment scheduling, generating, reviewing, and overriding process, which gives end users considerable control over their payment and vendor discount options. Its integration with PeopleSoft Workflow also provides for superior voucher and payment approval routing.

Using business unit features, organizations can set up separate areas of control. Multiple payables business units can roll up into a single general ledger business unit, allowing organizations to design their payables system around process requirements instead of accounting rules.

1.2.3 Accounts Receivable

With its Accounts Receivable module, PeopleSoft seeks to provide accounts receivable functionality and long-term credit management in one system. It includes the typical features of customer maintenance, receivables entry, and payment application. The intent is to minimize the routine transaction by automating as much as possible, so organizations can focus on exceptions.

It includes extensive customer management capabilities. Effective dating is integrated to track credit limit, risk classification, credit limit range, dispute status, and collection status. It can track an unlimited number of trade credit reports for each customer, allowing organizations to monitor trade credit information as it changes over time. Tricky payment options such as deductions, prepayments, and write-offs are designed to be easy.

1.2.4 Asset Management

PeopleSoft Asset Management aims to go beyond traditional asset management by providing capital appropriation planning and budgeting; projected depreciation on assets not yet purchased; multiple currencies for individual assets; customizable depreciation options; inventory and physical tracking functions; and maintenance, warranty, registration, and license tracking.

It supports an endless array of business unit organization options and multiple depreciation books, allowing multistate and international organizations to easily comply with varying accounting rule environments in a single system. Its integration with the other financial modules streamlines data entry and provides access to shared financial tables.

1.2.5 Billing

PeopleSoft Billing allows organizations to manage and carry out the process of invoicing their customers. It accurately applies surcharges, taxes, and discounts. It provides many of the same customer management advantages found in the accounts receivable module. It is closely integrated with the general ledger and accounts receivable modules to minimize data entry and share common, financial tables.

1.2.6 Inventory

PeopleSoft Inventory manages replenishment, order fulfillment, inventory levels, and warehouse space. It is closely integrated with the purchasing module to share common item definitions and to update inventory levels upon receipt of the goods. Its integration with project costing allows organizations to track distribution to various projects. Coupled with Workflow, it is capable of routing product definition approvals, order fulfillment requests, and shipping notifications.

1.2.7 Project Costing

Project Costing is a PeopleSoft financial module for tracking projects. It provides accurate totals of committed and actual costs. It includes powerful project cost analysis features. It supports allocations to and from the general ledger and between projects. Project Costing can define, maintain, and retire physical assets for full, life-cycle property management. It is well integrated with other PeopleSoft modules in order to minimize data entry and share common financial tables.

1.2.8 Purchasing

PeopleSoft Purchasing is a comprehensive purchasing module suitable for most organizations. It shares vendor and other information with accounts payable. It has a direct link to the asset management module to streamline entry of assets into the financial system. It is also closely integrated with the inventory module to leverage data entry productivity. It provides consistent information among purchase orders, vouchers, and payments, which streamlines the processing of purchase orders and their corresponding receipt and payment. It also includes the ability to manage vendor contracts. When integrated with Workflow, it can free purchasing units to focus on exception processing for significant efficiency gains.

1.3 The technology platform

While most client/server software companies build their applications using third-party tools, such as PowerSoft's PowerBuilder or third-generation programming languages such as C and COBOL, People-Soft delivers its own proprietary toolset, PeopleTools, with the applications. This can be both a boon and a deterrent. PeopleSoft has the ability to enhance the toolset in order to add functionality to its applications. Other financial application vendors are at the mercy of the toolset manufacturer or a slave to less-productive, third-generation compilers. As a result, PeopleSoft can bring new products and new releases to market in less time than most software vendors.

The foundation of PeopleTools is its online construction tools. These tools are used to define and maintain relational tables, build screens or panels, write specialized "PeopleCode" logic, define menus, and implement security around them. The Tree Editor offers users a way to hierarchically organize data into logical, multilevel branches for easy reporting and retrieval. Reporting is a multitool environment of "best-fit" tools for pulling different types of information to answer different types of questions. The reporting tools are aimed at the end user instead of programmers. PeopleSoft also provides data manipulation and maintenance tools. Workflow, a new tool to help automate the flow of work through an organization, is also included.

Experienced programmers will immediately recognize the inherent simplicity of PeopleTools. They facilitate rapid application development. In a single, iterative process, programmers can design, prototype, and build tables, panels, processes, and reports. Indeed, it is one of the reasons PeopleSoft is able to bring products to market quickly. This simplicity is traded off against a relative difficulty in completing the most intricate and complicated programming tasks. Programming purists, such as C++ zealots, may find the limitations in PeopleSoft and its paradigm to be stifling. Business analysts, however, will find them to be an ideal construction toolset for their applications. PeopleTools includes the following development "tools" in its integrated development environment.

1.3.1 Data Designer

Data Designer is used to define and maintain the definitions of relational tables, views, and work records. Database administrators can use it to generate data definition language statements to maintain the physical database environment. Data Designer includes an editor that allows programmers to write event-driven program modules called "PeopleCode" programs. The Data Designer associates PeopleCode programs with events for a given table definition.

1.3.2 Panel Designer

Panel Designer is a panel-building tool. Programmers choose fields from tables defined in Data Designer and place them on panels. Panel Designer supports multiple levels of tables, which are controlled by scroll bars.

1.3.3 Menu Designer

Menu Designer provides a means to logically group panels and organize them in menus. PeopleTools imposes no practical limit to the number of menus in a system, giving tremendous flexibility for organizations to design functional user interfaces for different groups of users. Typically, menus are organized around business processes.

1.3.4 Object Security

Object Security controls which PeopleTools objects users can manipulate. When using it, system developer access is assigned and controlled.

1.3.5 Help Designer

Help Designer is a client-based tool used to create and maintain online help text.

1.3.6 Operator Security

Operator Security is a tool for administering security for PeopleSoft applications. It provides operator classes, users that are assigned to classes, and other typical security features. When used in conjunction with Menu Designer, end user configuration management is simple yet powerful.

1.3.7 Tree Manager

With Tree Manager, financial staff can visually describe hierarchies of corporate data. Tree Manager is useful for showing hierarchical data such as organizational charts and charts of accounts.

1.3.8 Workflow

Workflow allows organizations to define business processes, including roles and routing. It can map information from external systems such as forms and email back into PeopleSoft. These processes appear as work lists on the menu of specific operators, where they are available for process and routing to the next operator.

1.3.9 Process Scheduler

Process Scheduler is a rich process-scheduling system. With it, operations staff controls the offline or batch programs or series of programs. It allows schedule recurring, one time or ad hoc, of multistep jobs at various process servers.

1.3.10 Data manipulation tools

PeopleSoft ships with tools to manage your applications and data. Application Upgrader facilitates the migration of customizations to production. It is also used to apply new releases of PeopleSoft from the vendor. Data Mover provides a platform-independent means for moving data between database management systems, archiving data and executive SQL statements against various databases. Import Manager can be used to load data from external systems into PeopleSoft applications. The Import Manager processes the data against specific types of PeopleCode, simplifying the editing process. Mass Change is used to update entire sets of data in a single operation.

1.3.11 Reporting tools

PeopleSoft reporting is an environment of its own. A variety of reporting tools is included, which are each designed to answer a specific type of

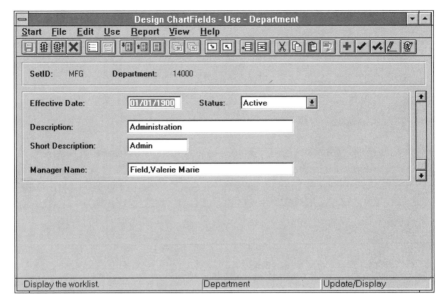

Figure 1.2 Effective dating panel

question about your data. These tools are integrated with the Process Scheduler, providing a robust, operational reporting strategy.

1.4 Distinguishing characteristics

1.4.1 Effective dating

All PeopleSoft applications utilize effective dating (see Figure 1.2). Relational tables, which may inherently change over time, include two additional fields as part of their key structure. Effective date and effective status combine to create rows of data having specific values—including whether they are active or inactive—for specific dates. This methodology defines the row with the greatest effective date less than or equal to the current date as the current row. All rows dated prior to that are considered historical, and all rows dated later are future rows. In this way, PeopleSoft preserves the "look" of the data over time.

Suppose an organization has a department "0001" called "News Publications," which posts transactions to the general ledger. Due to restructuring of the company, department 0001 is renamed "Publicity Services." In a traditional system, all reports, irrespective of the dates pulled from the general ledger, will show the new department name. With effective dating, the report will pull the row from the department table having the greatest effective date less than or equal to the date of the general ledger data. The correct description can be easily joined with the corresponding dated rows from the general ledger. Effective dating also gives end users the flexibility of entering future date information so as to minimize the impact of timing on changes made to their system.

1.4.2 Flexibility

PeopleSoft Financials, as delivered by the vendor, is only a starting point. The software exists to assume the unique characteristics of each organization. It is heavily table-driven. Its "Set ID" and "Business Unit" design provides support for organizations having multiple sets of books and different chart fields. Chart fields in PeopleSoft Financials are nearly limitless. The product ships with a chart field set of Business Unit, Account, Department, Project ID, and other elements to facilitate currency, statistics, and interunit accounting. However, it is expected that organizations will analyze their own businesses, strategic plans, and reporting needs to determine chart field requirements. PeopleSoft includes features that make chart field customization a matter of days rather than a matter of months.

It supports international currencies for international organizations or organizations that buy and sell internationally. Even the closing process is flexibible and designed to allow multiple runs before accepting the final close. Indeed, flexibility is one of the defining points of PeopleSoft Financials.

1.4.3 Integration

PeopleSoft Financials is a well-integrated set of software modules. Despite having released the modules somewhat sequentially since 1993, PeopleSoft has achieved a high level of consistency and integration. All financial modules are built with the common PeopleTools toolset. The company follows its own GUI design standard, which gives all the modules a common look and feel. In addition, the modules are implemented as a single relational database. This gives end users a single sign-on and an integrated environment. PeopleSoft also shares certain panels, tables, and programs among all modules.

This integration has a twofold benefit for PeopleSoft customers. First, the integrated system provides a single sign-on and look and feel for end users. Second, it means the products will mature more quickly, since the consistency and code reuse makes it easier for PeopleSoft to efficiently enhance the products. On the downside, organizations may become embroiled in political strife as system control issues are negotiated. It is not uncommon for certain financial functions to report to different senior management, and it can be a logistical problem as well as a human resources problem to define the system support responsibilities. Although the modules are designed for integration, they can stand alone. Although it is not an optimal installation, some organizations have implemented general ledger on one platform and other financial modules such as accounts payable on another. While this wastes one of the software's strengths, it is technically feasible.

1.4.4 "Fat Client" software

By now you're already aware that PeopleSoft is a client/server architecture. You may not be aware that PeopleSoft is built using a "fat client" strategy. In simple terms, this means that PeopleSoft locates a large part of the programming logic in the workstation as opposed to locating it at the database server. This puts added importance on specific parts of the computing infrastructure and affects performance. Experts argue both sides of this performance issue. They question whether this strategy performs well enough to scale to large installations. While the jury still may be out on this, many Fortune 500 companies have already decided that it scales well enough for them.

For the implementation team, it is imperative that no weak link exists in the client/server path. This means that the workstation, the network, and the database all need to perform at peak levels for the system to perform at its best. It means that performance tuning is a tricky endeavor. For the end users, it offers the maximum possible control over and access to corporate data. The strategy to "push" the information to the farthest reaches of the organization means that end users have easier access to more information and with more data manipulation options. This is a boon for flat organizations with empowered workforces.

The emphasis on the workstation is something that organizations must understand if they are to properly set expectations and achieve success in using the software. It has serious limitations for heads-down data entry processes. Performance modeling and tuning become doubly important. Failure to identify performance problems and performance targets for key processes can have a serious negative impact on the organization and the project team.

1.4.5 Integrated software distribution

One of the most critical aspects of client/server software is to efficiently distribute software updates to the clients. The worst-case scenario finds the technical support staff visiting each workstation to apply software updates. Poor distribution strategy has actually killed numerous client/server software projects, because the organization could not carry the overhead required to support the end users. PeopleSoft gives organizations an excellent foundation on which to build their software distribution strategy.

Although it is not a complete solution, PeopleSoft's strategy provides automatic distribution of software updates for all online modifications—for example, suppose a new field is added to the account table and this field is added to the account maintenance panel. The next time an end-user accesses that panel, PeopleSoft will recognize that both the account table and the account maintenance panel have changed. It will automatically download the new version of both to the user's workstation. This will manifest itself as a slight delay (a few seconds) for the end user to access that panel. Once the update is applied, no more delays will be experienced. Report modification and major vendor upgrades still pose distribution challenges, but they occur much less frequently.

1.4.6 End-user orientation

It may seem logical that any financial application would be targeted toward the end users. A case could, however, be made that many financial applications are built for the organization and not for the individuals within the organization. Such is not the case for PeopleSoft. PeopleSoft strives to be user-oriented software. It is designed with the requirements of the end users in mind and is constructed with tools that give the end user access to the system. By pushing information to the farthest reaches of an organization, PeopleSoft seeks to arm the knowledge worker with the information he or she needs. With this end-user focus, PeopleSoft Financials can help equip organizations for battle in the Information Age and the twenty-first century.

1.4.7 Built to be customized

The PeopleTools platform offers an unprecedented degree of user customization for users of PeopleSoft Financials. Traditional systems require systems analysts and programmers to analyze and implement modifications or extensions to the vendor software. It is expensive and time-consuming and requires more programming expertise than business expertise. Conversely, PeopleTools is a development toolset designed so that business experts can build, customize, and extend applications. In fact, people with no programming experience can, in a matter of hours, build an application. Because of this, it is easy for organizations to make minor modifications to the base software and to extend the system to include functionality unique to their industry or corporate culture.

This capability is often a big selling point for potential customers; however, it should be noted that major system design changes are extremely complex and difficult to manage. Also, processes that must operate in batch, such as journal entry posting, are difficult to customize. Organizations must also keep in mind that each customization made to the base software must be reapplied when installing a version upgrade from the vendor. PeopleSoft provides tools to help automate upgrades, but the decisions still must be made individually concerning which customizations to reapply and which ones to skip. Still—more so than applications from most other vendors—PeopleSoft's financial applications can be efficiently tailored to individual organizations.

1.4.8 Great expectations

PeopleSoft has stormed onto the software scene with such amazing speed that the company can aptly be called a phenomenon. PeopleSoft's PeopleTools, in spite of what detractors might say about them, can be captivating in a demonstration. End users, who are searching for something, anything, to help them transform their organizations for the next century, seem to find a veritable fountain of youth in PeopleSoft. The company is young and energetic. The software is new and exciting, and, most of all, it puts the information where it belongs: with the business expertise that can use it. Because they see an opportunity to energize their businesses, end users are often extremely zealous toward PeopleSoft. This is a shift for many organizations, where technology has been dictated from a central information systems department.

In practice, PeopleSoft Financials provides enough tangible benefits once it is installed that end users embrace it and the company, warts and all. A visit to the annual user conference is akin to attending a religious revival. At every session and every party there are excited, upbeat, positive people—all with common interests. Even the technical staff is excited about the chance to work with leading-edge programming tools. Some of the most beneficial sessions are found in the technical tract sessions where network specialists, database administrators, and programmer analysts share ideas and tricks they've learned. Even the negatives at the conference become positives when PeopleSoft senior management addresses the entire conference in a closing session titled, "PeopleTalk Back." The negative feedback, along with positive visions of its customers, is turned into strategic plans for the next year. Everyone returns home rejuvenated and full of energy.

The enthusiasm surrounding PeopleSoft is a positive for them, but it can be an unforeseen landmine for organizations implementing the software. End users and executives see the promise and glitz surrounding the software. They see how easily it can be customized. They hear about "information at their fingertips." They've been told they are getting a new generation of software and that it will free them from the shackles of traditional, mainframe software. They are expecting miracles. The vision is impressive, but unless it is coupled with effective action to reach the vision, the organization and project team are simply dreaming. Implementing PeopleSoft applications is difficult and takes talented, experienced staff. If the implementation is less than perfect or if the timeline stretches too far, the project and implementation team become instant targets. It is critical to keep the perception of the end users and executives in mind when setting expectations and communicating project status.

1.4.9 Outstanding financial reporting

For financial customers, reporting is an obvious factor in choosing software. The strongest selling point of PeopleSoft Financials may be its reporting capabilities. Most organizations have financial systems that allow them to process and store financial transactions. By and large, these systems have focused on the transactions at the expense of the financial reporting. PeopleSoft reverses this strategy and frees organizations to easily analyze their financial information.

End users are no longer dependent upon computer programmers for answers to their financial questions. They can choose from a variety of easy-to-use tools for reporting. PeopleSoft's flagship reporting method is its nVision tool. nVision is an add-on to the Microsoft Windows-based spreadsheet, Microsoft Excel. Using that familiar accountant's software, end users can define and format financial reports by defining spreadsheets that pull data directly from the general ledger database. Its reporting is so capable and intuitive that some organizations have purchased PeopleSoft General Ledger for the sole purpose of populating it for reporting, while leaving their existing general ledger systems intact. It is probably the single most striking advantage of the PeopleSoft financials software suite.

1.5 Benefits of PeopleSoft Financials

In many ways, implementing any new software system brings the inherent benefits of filling missing business requirements. It provides some vision to the implementation team. It often leads the organization to rethink its business processes in order to better utilize the software. This reengineering helps business units to operate more efficiently and to attain an appropriate staffing level. A new software system can often free valuable time for technical staff, allowing them to concentrate on other strategic areas for the organization.

PeopleSoft Financials brings with it additional benefits—some of which can set in motion sweeping organizational change. Perhaps the most noticeable change it brings to an organization is the transfer of ownership of the applications from central information systems to the functional, financial department. Because it gives an unprecedented level of control and flexibility to the end users, organizations can leverage the expertise of central information systems for technical matters and functional areas for business expertise. It represents a shift from the traditional role of information systems, and it can be politically tricky to settle on the compromise. Organizations should tackle this problem from the beginning. It may take an executive order to settle the system ownership issues, and care should be taken to mind the relationship between the two sides. This will be essential to the success of the implementation. People-Soft Financials will attempt to push the information and control as far down in the organization as possible, and entrenched power structures will undoubtedly resist this transformation.

As this control and information finds its new home, another benefit will begin to materialize. End users will find that they have, at their fingertips, the power to answer questions they could never before answer. They will also find that the information is accessible in familiar tools such as spreadsheets. A funds management professional in charge of making sure that sufficient balances are available to cover daily payables checks can now effectively and efficiently forecast payments in order to maximize investment revenues. Over time, this "information empowerment" will free the organization from the shackles of hierarchical organization structure and give it flexibility and access to information so it can flourish in the Information Age. This kind of organizational thinking is just beginning to find its way into corporations, and it will not entrench itself easily. A PeopleSoft implementation can, however, begin to lay the groundwork for sweeping organizational revolution.

Another major benefit in PeopleSoft Financials is its extensibility. Because it is designed to be customized, the software can adapt readily to changes in the business climate. And because control and information are located in the same part of the organization where these changes can be anticipated, the company can respond more quickly. The opportunity to lay the foundation for a new type of organization—one that is more efficient and effective—is perhaps a benefit unique to PeopleSoft Financials.

1.6 Who should implement PeopleSoft Financials?

When an organization seeks to find a major software package, it must consider its own organizational culture to ensure the software fits. It also must guard against paying for functionality that may never be used. PeopleSoft has its unique benefits, but it does not fit in every organization. So who should implement PeopleSoft Financials?

To begin with, organizations that are changing the way they operate by reengineering their business will find an ally in PeopleSoft. Business process reengineering seeks to streamline workflows and maximize efficiency of a unit by replacing antiquated procedures with new ones. Reengineering seeks to justify each step in a business process in terms of cost/benefit for the unit. PeopleSoft's process orientation provides the framework to carry out this transformation. The integrated workflow helps to automate business procedures, too. And because PeopleSoft has excellent data access and reporting features, traditional control steps often can be eliminated—for example, one purchasing unit decided to increase its approval requirement for purchase orders from $500 to $2,500, saving the staff needless paper shuffling. By analyzing its paper flow, it determined that this dollar range accounted for 50 percent of all their paper flow. Further investigation revealed that they really added no value to the process. They merely shuffled papers. Occasionally, a purchase order clerk would notice an inconsistency and take action. By reengineering its business processes, the company improved service to its internal and external customers and cut costs. In addition, using PeopleSoft's reporting features, they could still query the data to look for exceptions or abuses and use the information to modify the behavior of the offending units. Often, this reengineering can reduce costs and help justify the purchase of the software to executive officers.

Another reason organizations might implement PeopleSoft is to decrease dependency on the central information systems unit. PeopleSoft really must be owned and operated by the end-user department. The information systems unit acts only as a technical expert and data guardian. In its most extreme scenerio, all systems analysis and programming work can be accomplished by the end users, all but eliminating dependency on information systems. When end users lead the way, some power will inevitably shift away from information systems, and PeopleSoft is an excellent vehicle to help this trend reach equilibrium for the organization.

From a technical perspective, organizations with old, transaction-based or file/screen-based technology will get a technical jump start by implementing PeopleSoft. Traditional programmers require a great deal of retraining to move into the new paradigms of software development such as object-oriented and client/server. This training can be time-consuming and expensive. PeopleSoft is less demanding compared with constructing client/server and object-oriented software in-house. It does, however, familiarize developers with graphical user interfaces, relational database design, event-driven programming, and end users' reporting tools. This gives developers a good base on which to build a complete set of software development skills for today's needs.

1.7 Implementation: a road map to success

We have seen some of the strengths of PeopleSoft Financials. We have looked at some of the excitement surrounding the software and the company. We've also seen how complex and highly visible it can be. Because a PeopleSoft implementation will attract an unusual amount of attention in an organization, it is imperative that the implementation be carefully managed. Mistakes are magnified and can snowball due to the intricacies and relative youth of the technology. They can spell disaster for the project or, worse, the careers of the project team. To guard against such mishap, organizations must attend to the factors critical to the project's success.

1.7.1 Know the technology

First, it is essential that the organization understands the technology of PeopleSoft. It must determine if the PeopleSoft vision can fit within its corporate culture. Other pitfalls include lack of infrastructure. Firms that are new to personal computing, local area networks, and client/server software may not have the technical infrastructure to support PeopleSoft. It takes skilled technicians to install, maintain, and tune client/server software throughout an organization and there is a general industry-wide shortage of these skilled professionals. Programming staff may be trained only in traditional, mainframe, transaction-based software practices. Introducing event-driven programs with graphical user interfaces built on relational data models can overwhelm some staff members. Organizations lacking expertise in these areas will find that the project startup will be slower and more difficult.

1.7.2 Ensure adequate training

As part of the project initiation, care and expense must be taken to ensure that key individuals receive appropriate training. The formal project team will need the most training, but support staff must also be included. Some people may require prerequisite training to prepare them for the leap to new technology before they can effectively absorb specific PeopleSoft training. The timing of the training is crucial and will require careful planning. It will be expensive to develop the skills for the implementation, and executives must be persuaded to pay the bill. If training is neglected, the project manager cannot accurately define the project timeline, because unpredictable delays will assail the project at unpredictable times. Client/server software is difficult to implement in a perfect world, and a lack of expertise in any of the key areas can kill a project before it even begins.

1.7.3 Develop an implementation strategy

In any software installation project, the project team can choose from a limitless number of implementation strategies. A strategy provides a common vision or pathway for the project team. It gives executive sponsors a means by which they can evaluate the status of the project and, if necessary, provide feedback to the project team for incorporation into the project plan. Because of the myriad organizational interrelationships and the complexity of the software in a PeopleSoft installation, it is even more critical that the project team establish and agree to embrace a specific strategy for the implementation.

The factors that make up the strategy comprise all the components of a project. The makeup of the project team, the implementation steps involved in the project, the risk assessment techniques, communication plans, and the project plan update mechanism all become part of the overall strategy. We'll discuss this topic in detail in a later chapter. Suffice it to say that without the entire implementation team functioning in harmony, the project is doomed to a life of meandering from one issue to another—never achieving deliverables and never reaching completion. Inevitably, project team members involved in this situation do not garner support of executive sponsors or of senior management. And while a definite, communicated strategy will not guarantee success, it minimizes the chance of a complete project failure.

1.7.4 Install the technology

Before the project team can begin to analyze the software closely and compare it to the organization's business requirements, the software must be available for use. The installation of the software may seem like a trivial task. Usually, PeopleSoft installation professionals will carry out the actual installation of the software as part of the contract. It will generally take two to three days to install and verify the installation if there are no major, unforeseen obstacles such as hardware limitations or failure. The steps involved in an installation are many and complex. Each time the organization wants to install an upgrade or perhaps a new database, these steps will be required. The appropriate people must be exclusively dedicated to this initial installation. It may require that quite a varying group of staff members work together, some for perhaps the first time. It is important that this group formally define the responsibilities and document the steps involved in the installation. It may be many months until the next installation, so documentation is essential.

1.7.5 Reengineer your business

In recent years, business process reengineering, or BPR as it has come to be known, has become somewhat of a buzz word in the information systems industry. Perhaps some people have heard of it and have a vague idea of its meaning, but they might find it difficult to explain it to someone. Countless books have been published on this subject and are available for the reader's consideration. This book will not go into great detail on BPR. An oversimplification, however, defines BPR as: Evaulate your current business requirements and workflows and streamline them to minimize delays and waste, maximize efficiencies, and provide better outputs to your customers—both internal and external.

Without BPR, implementing a new software system is foolhardy. It does little for an organization besides wasting time and spending money. When BPR is used in conjunction with a detailed evaluation of the software's capabilities and the business's operational and strategic needs, the result is better service to customers and greater efficiencies. In short, it is more with less—every manager's favorite mantra. The project team that accomplishes this oxymoron earns the favor and respect of executive management and becomes a target for rewards. BPR, together with the new software, can do just that.

1.7.6 Customize the software

Once the software has been installed and the business requirements defined, the project team ought to have a formal list of software modifications to make to the base software. I stress the importance of keeping this list to a minimum, but recognize that all organizations will want to customize this software to some degree. Assuming the BPR process created the specifications, this step in the implementation will be of predictable duration. That duration will be directly related to the number and complexity of these modifications. We will discuss how the modifications might be categorized and prioritized to facilitate reaching a specific target date.

Typically, these customizations will either be completed by central information systems staff or by programmers from a PeopleSoft implementation partner. PeopleTools offers a highly productive toolset for the developers. Organizations should see relatively fast completion times for modifications if the base software closely matches their business requirements from the outset.

1.7.7 Set up financial options

While the programming staff is customizing the software, the end users can begin to populate the tables that will be used to drive the processing of PeopleSoft financials. Each of the financial modules is extensively table-driven. Most of the settings will result from decisions made in the reengineering process and will simply need to be entered. At this same time, the security manager can begin to establish the profiles and build the security structures. This will be an iterative process.

1.7.8 Convert the data

Most organizations will have preexisting financial data which will need to be migrated into PeopleSoft as history. This data migration is commonly referred to as data conversion. Data conversion provides both a starting point for the new software and an appropriate history basis. Often, legacy software has no historical capabilities, and it could be argued that perhaps the new software could be brought up "empty"; however, financial reporting requirements normally span fiscal years. Before data conversion requirements can be solidified, the project team must analyze the reporting needs and which data the new software will need in order to meet those needs.

Data conversions range from nearly trivial to nightmarish. The project team must understand the data in the old system and the data structures in PeopleSoft. They can then map data elements from the old system into the PeopleSoft relational tables. End-user involvement will be crucial for this mapping process to be accurate and complete. A striking characteristic of the data mapping is usually an exponential increase in the complexity of the data structures in PeopleSoft. One company replaced an in-house, general ledger system with PeopleSoft General Ledger. The data conversion required the project team to map data from two VSAM files and one tape file layout into over 100 relational tables in the PeopleSoft system.

Production cutover   Production cutover is the most exciting part of a software installation project. Months and even years of planning and effort culminate to a single point in time when the new software will be "turned on." On many project plans, production cutover occupies a single day and is presented as a milestone. In truth, it usually goes something like this.

- Parallel testing is carried out until the project team is reasonably confident of the accuracy of the new software.

- The project team scrambles to tie up loose ends. Programming staff will usually work long weeks to prepare for the cutover date. Last-minute items that were overlooked will further tax the project team.

- End users scramble to finalize policy changes and inform the organization. They will have to ensure that critical staff is properly trained on the new software and procedures.

- The cutover date arrives and programming staff switches all appropriate processing to turn off the old software and turn on the new.

- The project team spends several days cleaning up problems and investigating unpredicted consequences of the cutover.

- Finally, all critical kinks have been worked out of the software and, while it is not perfect, it is stable and accurate.

- The project team then spends between a few weeks and a few months detoxing from the rigors of the implementation and folding in lower-priority tasks.

PeopleSoft will be no different from most production cutover stages except that it will involve more staff. The client/server nature and the end-user orientation of PeopleSoft will dictate the involvement of an array of expertise, including programming staff, end users, network technicians, and database administrators. It is essential that time is allocated for these support staff, or the project team may find itself unable to remove some of the obstacles that will befall the cutover phase.

Performance tuning   Usually, software will not perform at peak levels the day it is put into production. The project team will have far too many tasks to complete to have undergone thorough performance tuning. Poorly performing software reflects badly on the project team. It can lead to frustrated end users, who usually are not shy about expressing their opinions. The project plan must include time for performance tuning after the software has stabilized. Given that PeopleSoft is a distributed technology, performance tuning will carry more weight here than on a traditional legacy system. Performance might vary drastically from one day to the next or even one hour to the next depending on several factors.

- The workload on the database server machine
- The number of users logged into PeopleSoft
- The number of batch programs running against the database
- The amount of traffic on the network
- The configuration of the local workstations
- The database queries generated by different parts of the software

The intricacy of PeopleSoft's architecture will make performance tuning both more difficult and more important, but it is an essential part of the implementation and cannot be neglected.

1.7.9 *Manage relationships*

Installing a complex software suite is very much a team effort. Whatever the endeavor, team dynamics are critical to its success. More than a few talented, professional sporting teams have been undermined by conflict and have realized less than their potential. The same is true of software implementation teams. Team relationships, of course, include those between the actual members. Other relationships are between the team and senior management, end users, network technicians, database administrators, technical support staff, the vendor, and consultants. This book will examine the various relationships and offer strategies to help structure an efficient, successful team.

PeopleSoft Financials poses unique and significant implementation challenges. Organizations that take heed and prepare for these challenges will enjoy a more successful project. They will have happier executive sponsors and end users. They will enjoy the benefits of a well-thought-out and structured financials system, which will help them compete in the years to come. Following this road map cannot predict a specific level of success, but it will guard against the nightmare of a failed project. Careful study of these factors will lead the project team to make informed decisions and avoid the countless pitfalls that leading-edge technologies incur.

chapter 2

Technology

Beginning in the late 1980s, developers began to incorporate the personal computer and local area networks into their software systems. Until then, software was primarily designed to be contained completely on a single computer system. Let's take, for example, a general ledger system running on an IBM mainframe computer. It was written in the COBOL language. It was designed with five indexed files and used the CICS transaction system. To access the screens, the end user logged into the mainframe computer using a terminal emulator and invoked the CICS transaction for entering a journal. The entire program ran on the mainframe computer. The end user's terminal was used only to display the information. This flavor of software system was the norm and is still common in corporations today.

When the personal computer came to the corporate world, software companies concentrated on productivity tools, which gave capabilities to end users that they did not get with their centralized systems. Software such as word processing, spreadsheets, and databases gave end users the ability to manage their own departmental systems. The next wave of technology brought local area networks to these departments, tying these end users together in islands of LAN-based productivity environments. This seemed like a good deal for the end users. They had the freedom to fill their own computing needs without waiting months or even years for central information systems to address their priorities. These benefits were offset, however, by other problems, which organizations were slow to recognize.

First, the departmental systems were often developed iteratively by people who were not familiar with software development disciplines. By and large they reflected the current processes. They offerred productivity gains by automating manual processes, but they were installed without reengineering the processes themselves. As these small systems became more entrenched, departments became more closely tied to their processes, making it increasingly difficult to gain new efficiencies. Departments also found, sometimes the hard way, that these systems required support staff. Functions they took for granted with their centralized systems included backup and restore, disaster recovery, hardware maintenance and upgrade, end-user support, and software enhancements. Organizations began to find that they had developed redundant resources and expertise in these islands of data processing, as each department hired its own local area network manager.

It was also evident that much of the data tracked in these systems had become mission-critical—that is, organizations now relied on that data in order to be able to do business. These data were not easily accessible to other departments or to senior management. Without this information, executives had to formulate strategy without incorporating some of these data. During this same period, global economic pressures urged companies to work differently, reshaping their organizations to be more responsive to customer needs. This was typified by the Total Quality Management movement in the United States starting in the 1980s.

In spite of the negatives surrounding the growth of this isolated software, it had one significant and positive impact. It exposed the weaknesses of central information systems and brought to light the customer needs they were blatantly ignoring. In many ways it was resposible for the dismantling of the glass house mentality and a move to a focus on customer service by information systems professionals. To that end, it was a major ingredient in the establishment of the next paradigm in software systems: client/server.

Client/server software seeks to marry the control and stability of central information systems with the superior functionality and ease of use of PC-based software. The industry flooded the market with software development toolsets for designing and building client/server software. Tools such as PowerSoft's PowerBuilder, Gupta's SQLWindows, and ORACLE emerged as robust, full-featured client/server software development platforms. They were solid products upon which corporate software could be built, but they were still complex and required professional programmers. It was in this environment that PeopleSoft was born.

PeopleSoft, being a new company, did what few other software vendors have done. They developed the corporate vision and then sought to adopt a development platform that would support that vision. Specifically, PeopleSoft wanted to build and sell user-oriented software. That would require a powerful yet simple software development environment based on industry-standard operating environments. At that time, nothing of the sort could be found on the market, so PeopleSoft designed and built its own Microsoft Windows PeopleTools. It consists of a complete data processing platform, including online development, batch processing, reporting, and database management. (See Table 2.1.)

Table 2.1 PeopleTools Development Toolset

Processing Type	Tool
Application Definition Tools	Data Designer
	PeopleCode
	Panel Designer
	Menu Designer
	Object Security
	Help Designer
Batch and Database Tools	Process Scheduler
	Application Engine
	Import Manager
	Mass Change
	Data Mover
	Operator Security
	Application Upgrader
Information and Business Process Tools	Tree Manager
	Reporting Environment
	Workflow
Software Distribution	PeopleTools Objects Locations and PeopleTools Objects Locations

2.1 PeopleTools database structure

The physical, technical design of PeopleTools is fairly straightforward. Since the processing starts at the client, let's start there. The client workstation must run Microsoft Windows. As of version 5, both Windows NT and Windows 95 are supported. On the workstation, installers load the PeopleTools executables. In the early days of PeopleSoft, sales representatives took great delight in pointing out to potential customers that PeopleTools was made up of four C programs. That number has increased quite a bit, but PeopleTools is still a compact set of executable programs, which run on the client workstation. Depending on the database platform, various database programs, dynamic link libraries, and configuration files are also required at the client workstation. In addition, other dynamic link libraries and third-party software packages are shipped with PeopleTools and are loaded to the client workstation.

The only function the programs on the client workstation provide is access to build and execute PeopleSoft programs. The programs themselves do not truly reside on the workstation, although they are cached there in swap files, which we'll discuss later. The programs themselves, made up of PeopleTools objects (tables, panels, fields, queries, menus, etc.), are stored in special PeopleTools tables in the database—for example, when a developer creates a new record definition complete with fields, edits, and database attributes, the information about that record is stored in a PeopleTools table called PSRECDEFN. Panel information is stored in PSPNLDEFN and so on. A PeopleSoft database really consists of three separate types of tables. First, there are the database system tables. These are the tables that the relational database management system uses to keep track of the format and contents of the data it is storing. In IBM's DB2, for example, SYSTABLES is a database table that DB2 uses to define and track the tables in a given database. The second type is known as the PeopleTools tables. In the simplest terms, the PeopleTools tables define how the application will look. It stores information about the format, layout, and programming logic of the application. The third type of tables is the data tables. These are the tables that actually store the organization's information. An example of a data table is the LEDGER table, which stores periodic totals posted against specific chart field combinations. (See Figure 2.1.)

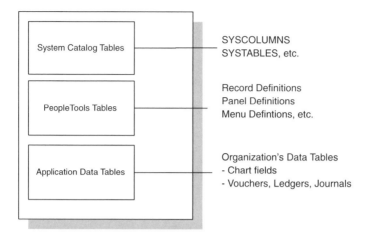

Figure 2.1 Types of tables in a PeopleSoft database

It is important to be aware of this distinction among the tables. The relationship between the executable programs on the client workstation is critical. In order to move to a new release of PeopleTools, the installer must load a new set of executables to the workstation. He or she must also update the layout of the PeopleTools tables—for example, suppose we wish to upgrade to PeopleTools 5.0 from PeopleTools 3.1. First, we would install the executables at the workstation. Next, we would need to run some SQL scripts, which would add, change, and delete some of the fields in the PeopleTools tables. It might even convert some of the values in them. These new PeopleTools fields support the new features of version 5.0. Attempting to run client executables against PeopleTools tables of a different version will result in SQL errors and the software will not run. In summary, when we update PeopleTools, we change the *format* of the PeopleTools tables.

Contrast this with the activity when we modify our *application.* Suppose we want to add a new field to the Accounts panel. Using PeopleTools, we would bring up the design for our Accounts panel, place the new field on the panel, and save the panel. This would update the contents of the row(s) of data in the panel definition tables pertaining to our Accounts panel. So, when we update our application software, we change the *contents* of the PeopleTools tables. The PeopleTools version impacts the format of the PeopleTools table. The application software version impacts the contents of the PeopleTools tables. This can be a confusing difference, because installers often upgrade PeopleTools and the Application together. It is an important concept for developers to understand.

This design causes serious performance concerns. Since the application programs are all stored in the database, this means that each time a user invokes a panel, the workstation's executables must query the database and retrieve the specifications for that panel before they can display them for the user. For complex panels and programs, this can be a lengthy process. A single panel group might be made up of ten or more panels with hundreds of objects. It can take from several seconds to a few minutes to completely retrieve all of these objects from the database, depending upon the configuration. PeopleTools addresses this by storing copies of the objects on the end user's workstation in "swap files." To understand the logistics of this, we must briefly explain the concept of version numbers.

Each PeopleTools object in a PeopleSoft database includes a version number field, called VERSION. The database includes a global, current version number, which is incremented each time a change is made to a PeopleTools object. in our Account panel example above, when we saved the modified panel, PeopleTools would retrieve the current version number, increment it by one, set the value of the VERSION field to that new number, and then save the panel definition to the database. When an end user invokes a panel, PeopleTools first compares the version number of the panel stored in the database with that of the panel definition stored locally in the swap files. If they are the same, the local swap files will be used. Only when the versions are different does PeopleTools retrieve the definition from the database and rewrite it to the swap files. In this way, PeopleSoft circumvents the potential performance problems associated with this design.

2.2 Application definition tools

2.2.1 Data Designer

Data Designer is the heart and soul of PeopleTools. With it, the underlying data model of the software is actualized. PeopleSoft Financials is implemented using a relational database management system. Relational databases simplify data access by abstracting the physical layout from the logical. To retrieve data from a nonrelational database, programmers must meticulously code a program to navigate the database and pick fields from specific locations in particular files. With relational databases, data are retrieved by selecting named fields, called columns, from specific file names, called tables. The data access language used to access relational databases is called Structured Query Language, or SQL. A sample SQL program to access a description from the account table might look like this.

```
Select Account_Code, Account_Descr
From Account_Table
Where Account_Code < "0145"
```

Data Designer further abstracts the design of the relational model by storing record definitions in PeopleTools tables. Using Data Designer, developers define the layouts of all records in the system. Each record layout includes the following information.

- Field attributes such as format, length, name, and description
- Key structures, default values, and field audit requirements
- Various edits such as required, prompt table
- Any programming logic, called *PeopleCode*

Data Designer also defines the virtual records, or work records, and relational views. Views are designed identically to tables except that they are designated as views. The view creation text is stored with the record definition. (See Figure 2.2.)

Since an early version of PeopleTools, Data Designer has had the capability to generate the SQL database definition language commands to create and alter the tables, views, and indexes it creates. With the release of version 5, PeopleSoft has added substantial capabilities for storing database object information to aid database administrators. It is effectively a repository of database definition information suitable for database administrators in most cases. It does not include a data modeling tool, and many database administrators rely on modeling products to help create the database objects. However, in spite of this one shortcoming, Data Designer is sufficient to serve as the repository of database definition information for database administrators.

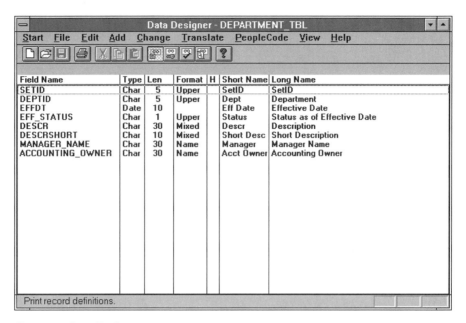

Figure 2.2 Data Designer screen capture

2.2.2 *PeopleCode*

PeopleCode is PeopleSoft's proprietary programming language. As with all programming tools, developers must have a way to code specific logic using programming syntax. With PeopleTools, developers tie programming logic to database fields on specific records defined in Data Designer. PeopleTools is an event-driven system. This means that programming logic is invoked in response to specific events in the application. Traditional programming is structured so that programs execute from the beginning until they reach a stop command in the program. The nature of the graphical user interface necessitates the use of event-driven programming. (See Figure 2.3.)

PeopleCode responds to numerous events corresponding to different types of PeopleCode. Each event occurs at a different point—for example, when a user presses the Save button, the panel processor looks for any records with Save-Edit PeopleCode definition. It invokes those code modules it finds and processes them before moving to the next event, Save-PreChange. (See Table 2.2.)

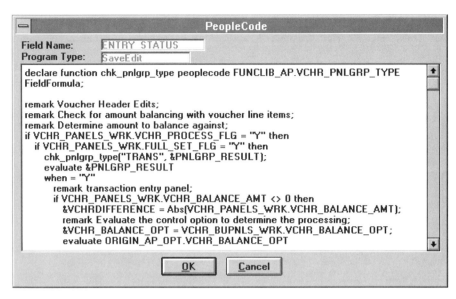

Figure 2.3   PeopleCode screen capture

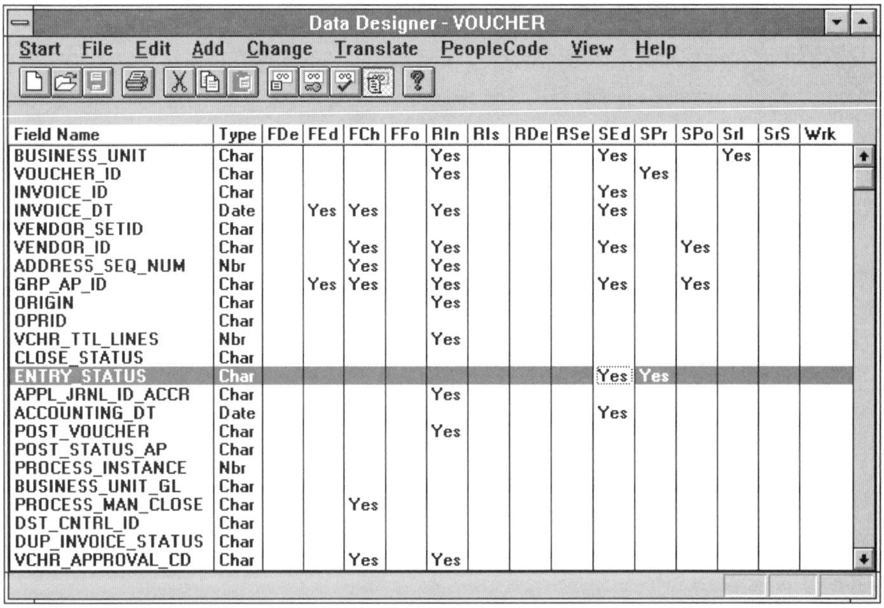

Figure 2.4   Record definition PeopleCode display (voucher table)

Table 2.2 PeopleCode Type Descriptions

PeopleCode Type	Description
Field-Change	Invoked when the value of a field changes
Field-Default	Invoked when a field is newly initialized
Field-Edit	Invoked when a field loses focus
Field-Formula	This type of PeopleCode is used to store common procedures. It does not execute in response to any particular event. It must be specifically called from another PeopleCode type.
Row-Delete	Invoked when a row of data is deleted from a panel
Row-Init	Invoked when a new row of data becomes the active row on a panel
Row-Insert	Invoked when a new row of data is inserted onto a panel
Row-Select	Invoked when a row of data is selected on a panel
Save-Edit	Invoked when the Save button is pressed on a panel and before changes are saved to the database
Save-PostChange	Invoked after the changes are committed to the database
Save-PreChange	Invoked after Save-Edit but before the changes are committed to the database
Search-Init	Invoked when a record is accessed as a search record for a panel
Search-Save	Invoked when the search dialog box is saved to locate records for a panel

The Data Designer stores these types of PeopleCode on a record-by-record basis (see Figure 2.4). The record definition for the ACCOUNT_TBL, for example, is defined as follows.

```
ACCOUNT    CHAR(4)
ACCOUNT_DESCR CHAR(30)
```

Suppose that Save-Edit PeopleCode is defined for the ACCOUNT_DESCR field to ensure that it begins with the letter "A" or "B." If it does not, the program will issue an error message and return focus to the ACCOUNT_DESCR field for correction. With PeopleTools, everywhere in the system that the ACCOUNT_TBL is used, this same PeopleCode will execute at Save-Edit time. In other words, the programming logic follows the record definition throughout the system, minimizing the amount of programming required through the system. PeopleCode, together with Data Designer, provides a powerful and yet remarkably simple program development foundation.

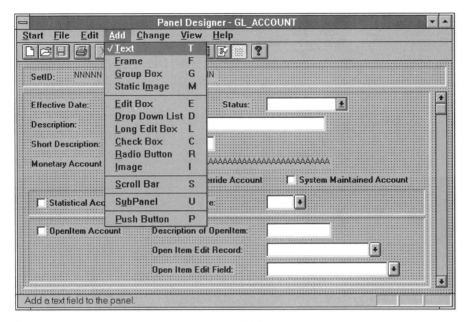

Figure 2.5 Panel Designer capture (account table)

2.2.3 Panel Designer

Any software system needs a mechanism for interacting with users. The most common user interface type is the screen. Screens are composed with fields from the database, and changes to the screen are updated in the underlying database tables. In PeopleTools, screens are called panels, and they are designed and built using the Panel Designer. At run time, the Application Processor translates the characteristics of panels into SQL statements to access and update the database. It includes all of the typical screen design features, but its capabilities go beyond those of traditional screen builders. (See Figure 2.5.)

Using Panel Designer's drag-and-drop interface, developers place fields from tables in the database onto the the panel in various locations. It supports several types of fields for an impressive array of design and usability options. (See Table 2.3.)

Table 2.3 Field Types Supported by Panel Designer

Panel Field Type	For Database Field Types
Check Boxes	Yes/No
Drop-down List Box	Character with Lookup Values
Edit Box	Number, Date/Time, Character, Yes/No
Image	Image
Long-Edit Box	Variable-Length Character Field
Radio Button	Character with Lookup Values

Subpanels are a feature that allows developers to define sets of fields that commonly appear grouped together. They can define them once, as a subpanel, and simply place the subpanel on individual panels. The Application Processor will pull the subpanel fields into the panel. This is a timesaver for fields that commonly appear together, such as ADDRESS, CITY, STATE, ZIP.

Besides the database fields, developers can choose from the typical array of graphical objects to enhance a panel's look and feel. Text fields, frames, group boxes, and static images can be sized and placed on panels, as with most GUI design tools. Panel Designer, beginning with version 5, has font and color selection options putting it on a par with other toolsets. Besides these typical features, Panel Designer has industrial-strength features, which make it suitable for corporate software.

Panel groups   Typically, several relational tables containing numerous fields are related to form a "set" of information. Usually, with traditional screen designers, these data have to be spread across multiple screens. Users must carry out multiple transactions to properly update all of these related data. The proliferation of data modeling techniques and relational databases has exacerbated this problem. Panel Designer's panel grouping features allow developers to combine multiple, related tables into a logical group of panels that appear together. Users cycle through the panels using an option on the panels' toolbar or by using a keyboard function key. The panel groups are treated as a single, logical panel, and the fields on all the panels are saved together when the user presses the Save button.

Panel groups allow the online software to be designed around business processes instead of individual data files, as with traditional software. This is an important feature, because one of the weaknesses of client/server software is performance. The first impression of client/server screens is that they are relatively slow as compared with character-based transaction-processing screens. With panel groups, PeopleTools can achieve better overall performance because end users concentrate on units of work instead of individual screens.

F4 prompt In concert with the Data Designer, Panel Designer gives users excellent data prompting features. Any field on a record can be tied to a prompt table—another table with valid values and other attributes. Prompt tables can be either actual tables or database views, giving excellent flexibility.

Scroll levels PeopleTools supports multiple levels of data per panel group, which are controlled by scroll bars—for example, suppose we have a vendor table and a vendor address table. Let's assume that each vendor row can have multiple address rows corresponding to various locations. A single panel or panel group to maintain vendors and their addresses could consist of the vendor information at the top. The multiple addresses for the vendor at the top of the panel would be below the vendor information, and their occurrences would be controlled by a scroll bar. Panel Designer supports multiple scroll levels, called nested scrolls. Combined with the various PeopleCode event types, developers have a powerful set of programming and processing options for executing procedural logic. Using scroll levels, PeopleTools panel groups are capable of manipulating vast amounts of data, spanning numerous tables, to support complex business processes. (See Figure 2.6.)

Process and command buttons Process and command buttons can be placed on panels to carry out specific actions when pressed. The developer ties PeopleCode or Workflow to the pushbuttons. Options for pushbuttons include jumping to a different panel automatically and executing the next step in a process definition. PeopleSoft's Payable Pay Cycle Manager panel uses a process pushbutton to help end users through the sequential steps required to generate and print payables checks.

In summary, PeopleTools Panel Designer is a capable, effective platform for organizations to build on. It does not offer developers the

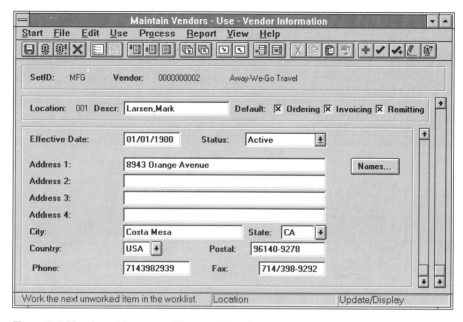

Figure 2.6 Vendor address panel for scroll levels

maximum flexibility and capability found in native Windows API programming, but it more than makes up for that weakness with major productivity and ease-of-use improvements. PeopleSoft also builds its software based on usable GUI design standards. This is something organizations can simply adopt—saving the time and effort of developing those standards for themselves.

2.2.4 Menu Designer

Menu Designer is used to organize the panels produced using Panel Designer into logical groups for access by end users. PeopleSoft menus typically cluster logically related panels and panel groups together to form a *window*. A group of windows make up the entire online data entry portion of a PeopleSoft system. All available windows appear as options on the PeopleTools Start menu. A window contains several online processing options, which are accessible via its Use menu. Each of these options on the Use menu contain one panel group as well as various other information needed by the Application Processor to navigate through the system. Windows will also often have both a Process menu

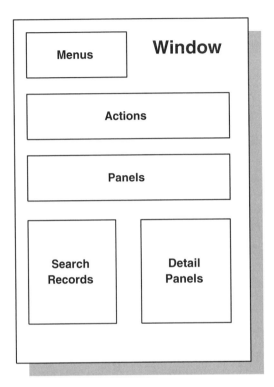

Figure 2.7 Components of PeopleTools windows

and a Reports menu and sometimes other menus such as Tables to group lookup tables. Process menus contain programs that update the database in a batch mode and are related to the window's logical function. The Reports menu will consist of reports that are related to the window's logical function. (See Figure 2.7.)

Let's take a look at a sample menu (see Figure 2.8). Suppose we wish to work with data pertaining to vendors with which an organization transacts business. Assume we want to enter a vendor, approve it, and then print a report of all vendors on system. Our steps would be as follows. (See Figure 2.9.)

- From the Start menu on the startup window, we would select the Work with Vendors window. This would invoke the vendors' window with its own menu.
- From the Use menu on the Work with Vendors window, we would select the Maintain Vendors panel group.

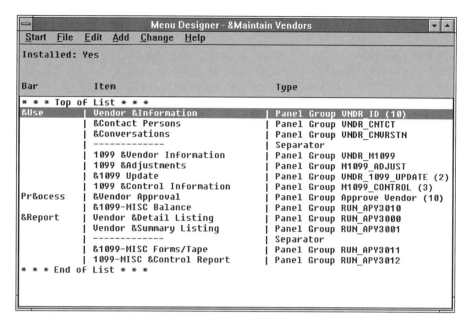

Figure 2.8 Menu screen capture (work with vendors)

- Once the panel group is selected, we must choose an action. In this case, we want to create a new vendor, so we would choose the Add action.

- The system would prompt us for the keys of the new vendor via a dialog box. Normally, we'd choose "NEXT" for the Vendor ID and press the OK button to invoke the panel group. The first panel in the group would then display on our Work with Vendors window.

- We would complete the data on the first panel and then cycle through the remaining panels, filling out the appropriate information on each panel.

- Next, we would press the Save button on the toolbar. Assuming we made no entry errors, the new vendor would be saved to the database. We would then be ready to enter another vendor or carry out another task. In this case, we want to approve the vendor so it can be paid.

- From the Process menu on our Work with Vendors window, we would next select Approve Vendors.

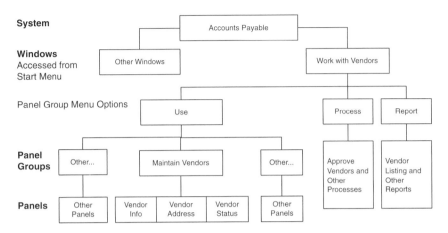

Figure 2.9 Flow chart showing steps to enter and approve a vendor

- The system would display the Approve Vendors process panel. We would enter the required information and then press the Run button on the toolbar. The vendor approval program would be started and would run in the background.

- When our approval program completed, we would then select Vendor Listing from our Reports menu on the Work with Vendors windows. Running that report would require the same steps used to run the vendor approval program. The only difference is that it would produce a report for us to print.

This entire navigation process occurred within the context of a single PeopleTools window. We accessed a total of three panel groups made up of five separate panels, but they all related to vendor processing. This navigation seems a little bizarre at first, but its complexity becomes second-nature for the average user. The combination of Actions and Panels provides a good deal of flexibility to design and construct the system's navigation, and its structure makes it fairly easy to adhere to the menu design standards.

A powerful, and perhaps most important, feature of Menu Designer is its Search Record capability (see Figure 2.10). Search records are pseudorecords that control which rows of data are passed to a panel group for editing. The basis of search records begins in the Data Designer (see Figure 2.11). Fields entered in a record definition can be optionally assigned the search key attribute. Then, whenever that record is associated with a

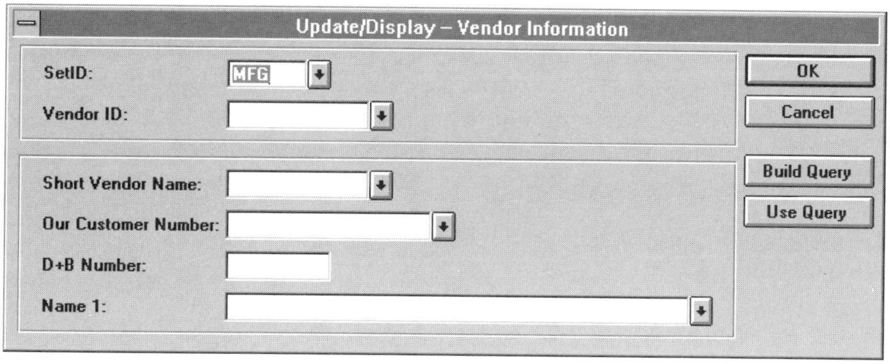

Figure 2.10 Search record capture (use vendor search record)

panel group as its search record on a menu definition, those fields are used to select which row(s) the user wishes to edit. Continuing with our vendor example, let's examine how search records are used. In Data Designer, suppose our vendor table includes the following fields.

```
SETID                  CHAR(5)
VENDOR_ID              CHAR(10)
VENDOR_NAME_SHORT      CHAR(10)
AR_NUM                 CHAR(10)
DB_NUM                 CHAR(10)
NAME1                  CHAR(30)
VENDOR_STATUS         CHAR(1)
VENDOR_PERSISTENCE    CHAR(1)
ENTERED_BY            CHAR(8)
```

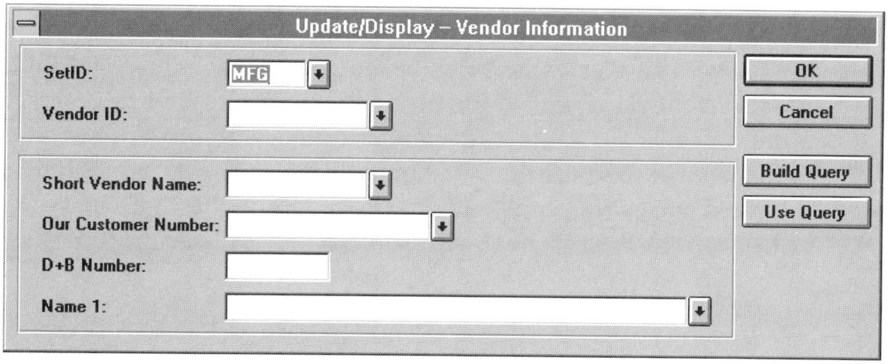

Figure 2.11 Data Designer screen capture (vendor search)

Suppose also that we identify SETID, VENDOR_ID, VENDOR_NAME_SHORT, AR_NUM, DB_NUM, NAME1, and VENDOR_STATUS as search key fields. We can create a SQL view called VENDOR_VW with the following SQL statement.

```
CREATE VIEW PS_VENDOR_VW
(SETID, VENDOR_ID, VENDOR_NAME_SHORT,
AR_NUM, DB_NUMBER, NAME1, VENDOR_STATUS)
AS select  a.setid,
           a.vendor_id,
           a.vendor_name_short,
           a.ar_num,
           a.db_number,
           a.name1,
           a.vendor_status
     from   ps_vendor a;
```

In Menu Designer, if we define VENDOR_VW as the search key for our Maintain Vendors panel group, something very convenient will occur. When we access that panel group, the system will display a dialog box prompting us to enter values in these fields. Assuming we are searching for a particular vendor to update, we can enter search criteria so the Application Processor can retrieve a subset of rows from which we can select. Suppose we know neither the VENDOR_ID nor VENDOR_NAME_SHORT but we do know that NAME1 begins with "All." We can enter "All" in the Vendor Name (NAME1) field and press OK. The system will return a list of all vendors whose names begin with "All." We then select our specific row from the list, and it will be passed to the Maintain Vendors panel group for our use. Search records are not limited to database tables. Views, which are logical groups of tables with specific where criteria, can be used as search records. Add to this the capability to branch from the search dialog box directly into a database query, and end users have extremely flexible and simple techniques for finding their data in the database. To further help end users find the correct rows of data, developers tie detail panels to panel groups. To see more detail about a row of data in our example above, we would highlight a row of data in our list of vendors and press the Detail button. The system would display a read-only panel with additional details about that row of data.

2.2.5 Help Designer

It is a good idea to include online help in any new software. Traditionally, programmers developed the software and put it in production before any effort went into documentation. When documentation was finally produced, it was most likely a hardcopy manual, written by the programmer. This documentation was never really useful for end users. A quick thrill for helpdesk operators has always been to ask the end user if he or she has looked up the error message in the system manual. Usually, there would be a noticeable pause, and the user would deny ever having seen such a manual. Getting people to read the words on the computer screen is somewhat of a coup, but thick, boring, confusing manuals simply are not used. Fortunately, PeopleTools has a way to develop online help.

Developers can choose from two types of online help. The first is to create help using the Help Designer. These help descriptions are stored as part of the PeopleTools help database tables. Help text can be tied to specific panels, records, or field definitions for context-sensitivity. Its biggest strength is ease of use. The other method is to use the Microsoft Windows Help System and build powerful, indexed, hypertext help. Using Data Designer and Panel Designer, the Help System can tie specific contexts to panels, records, and fields for a very powerful and flexible Help System. While this option is more capable, it is also more complex. Together, these two methods will fill nearly all online help requirements.

2.3 Batch processing environment

In typical fashion, PeopleSoft has set out to combine separate, best-of-breed tools and marry them with their own technologies to quickly provide a robust and flexible batch-processing environment. It seems that most software is judged on the online portion of the software; in fact, most software demonstrations focus on this exclusively. In other words, end users are typically most interested in how *they* will interact with the database. The user interface is justifiably given critical weight in the selection process for software. However, information systems professionals know that it is the batch, or background, processes that are the workhorses of software systems. What good would an accounts payable system be if it had an outstanding online user interface, but could not reliably produce accurate payments and general ledger transactions? It would look great in a demonstration, and payables clerks would achieve notable levels of efficiency; however, when vendors began to clamor over incorrect payments and auditors found blatant accounting errors, the payables department would quickly lose that productivity.

These batch shortcomings might not be visible in software demonstrations, and potential customers should rely on site references from installed clients to judge the sureness of the software's background processing. What *is* visible in a demonstration is the platform on which the batch processes are built. PeopleSoft utilizes technologies to implement batch processes. The actual programs are coded in one of two languages: COBOL or SQR. In order to control the scheduling and running of these batch programs, PeopleSoft provides a process-scheduling tool appropriately dubbed Process Scheduler.

2.3.1 *Application engine*

The PeopleSoft Application Engine is a relatively new tool for executing offline programs. It is at first very confusing. Using PeopleSoft panels, the programmers create a batch program by defining the steps to be carried out. SQL statements, queries, mass changes, procedural code, and COBOL subroutines are all candidates for a given program step. The Application Engine's integration with PeopleTools is impressive, but it is a proprietary tool. COBOL and SQR are not PeopleSoft products, but Application Engine is (see Figure 2.12). It is not common for application vendors to package their own proprietary batch programming language, so there are some advantages and disadvantages.

First, by including these batch programs completely within the database, programmers can build, run, and debug programs from within the PeopleTools environment. Application Engine supports PeopleSoft's effective dating, which documents program functionality over time. Developers can deactivate a step of code on a particular date without deleting the step. It is still available for future use, if needed. And because Application Engine accesses the PeopleSoft Data Designer data dictionary to determine how to process fields, batch programs written using it are isolated from field changes. COBOL and SQR programs have

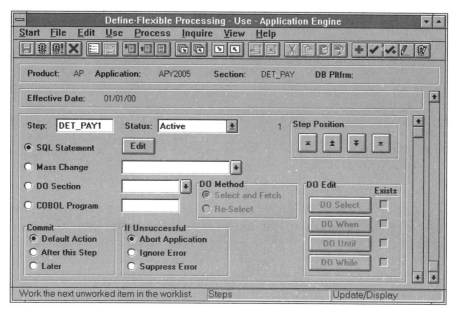

Figure 2.12 Application Engine screen capture

to be modified over time, because their field definitions are statically defined in the programs.

A disadvantage, however, is that it is a new language. The implementation team already has a steep, steep learning curve in front of it, and Application Engine will not ease that pain. It is also proprietary, which means that its components cannot be readily shared with applications outside of PeopleSoft financials. On the whole, however, it is an effective means to create set-processing, offline programs that are easy to maintain and have maximum portability.

2.3.2 *PeopleSoft COBOL programs*

The COBOL programming language was originally developed as a business-oriented programming language. Its existence was supposed to allow nontechnical people to write computer programs. That goal never materialized, but COBOL, despite its numerous shortcomings, went on to become the most prevalent programming language for business applications. New-world developers often think of COBOL as less capable and tend to choose C or C++ as their programming language of choice. Its bad reputation is not caused by lack of capabilities as much as by simple misuse. Much of the bad COBOL code in the world was written in the 1960s and 1970s, when a majority of programmers lacked formal training in information systems practices. PeopleSoft leverages COBOL's strengths of file processing and business programming, using it for the most complex and intricate batch processes.

The design of the COBOL programs is quite good from a developer's point of view, but quite complex for the organizations installing them. A single batch COBOL process, such as general ledger journal posting, may be made up of 50 or more separate COBOL programs. This is because PeopleSoft uses individual components, which are called by the main programs and its subprograms. Each component is a small program in itself. That makes defining its inputs, processes, and outputs an easy task. Testing small programs is comparatively simple, and modifying a process need only be done once, in the component; all other programs using it will automatically gain the updated functionality. In that way, PeopleSoft can effectively manage its COBOL code and efficiently apply fixes and enhancements. For organizations, however, it makes it extremely difficult to understand and follow programming logic, because they don't have access to detailed design specifications of the programs and components. For this reason, PeopleSoft strongly discourages organizations from modifying the COBOL programs.

PeopleSoft COBOL programs have another unusual characteristic. The SQL statements that are used to retrieve and update the database are themselves stored in database tables. The SQL statements executed against the database turn out to be dynamic SQL, making the programs even more difficult to follow. This strategy does offer PeopleSoft a degree of platform portability that benefits all clients. SQL dialects vary with each database management system, and minimizing the static SQL statements to those that retrieve the dynamic SQL makes it easier for them to manage the COBOL source code. So, what is of great benefit to PeopleSoft is a hindrance to the organizations installing their software. In most cases, however, the COBOL is compiled and runs as is, or with minimal client modifications.

2.3.3 PeopleSoft SQR processes

For most of the background update processes, PeopleSoft uses MITI Structured Query Report Writer, or SQR. SQR is a flexible SQL reporting language. Its basic programming paradigm builds program processing around any sort of SQL statement. Within the context of that SQL statement, specific subroutines can be called for each row of data in the main select. SQR is portable across PeopleSoft's database platforms and operating systems. (See Figure 2.13.)

```
...
!-----------------------------------------------------
-!
!Select 1996 Current Balance from Ledger              !
!-----------------------------------------------------
-!
begin-procedure Extract-Vendors
begin-SELECT
BUSINESS_UNIT
LEDGER
DEPTID
SUM(POSTED_TOTAL_AMT) &POSTED_TOTAL

  DO Write-Vendor-file

FROM PS_LEDGER
WHERE FISCAL_YEAR = 1996 AND ACCOUNTING_PERIOD > 0
GROUP BY BUSINESS_UNIT, LEDGER, DEPTID

end-SELECT
end-procedure Extract-Vendors

  !-------------------------------------------------!
  ! Write Vendor File                               !
  !-------------------------------------------------!
begin-procedure Write-Vendor-File

    do Format-Number(&POSTED_TOTAL, $out,
ô9999999999999.99')

WRITE 1 From &BUSINESS_UNIT:5
             ô,'
             &LEDGER:10
             ô,'
             &DEPTID:9
             ô,'
             $out:22
```

Figure 2.13 Sample SQR program section

PeopleSoft uses SQR extensively for batch programs. SQR programs are less tricky to modify than the COBOL source. Some customers modify only a few programs, and others modify them extensively and add their own SQR programs to supplement the processing PeopleSoft provides. They ship a base set of common routines, which programmers can include in their programs. Date formatting, number formatting, lookup table processes, and other common routines need not be recoded. For most batch programs, SQR offers sufficient performance and functionality.

2.3.4 Process Scheduler

Organizations with mainframe computers long ago recognized the value of automatically running programs with job-scheduling software. Production control staff only had to load the schedule of jobs (a job is a set of programs that run together as a single unit of processing), their dependencies, and error-processing options into the scheduler, and the programs would start automatically when all required conditions for them were met. The alternative was to schedule all these offline programs manually each night. This is labor-intensive and is more prone to errors. PeopleSoft needed a way to schedule programs and jobs and to integrate that scheduling with its software. That is the function of the Process Scheduler.

The Process Scheduler provides a set of database tables and online panels in which organizations can define all of their offline processing programs and jobs. By using database variables and environment variables to resolve a program execution time, organizations have excellent flexibility to define and implement an intricate array of process servers and program execution schedules. It supports multistep jobs, recurring jobs, and remote submission to servers and has the ability to run programs and jobs on client workstations as well. By integrating it with the application itself, it provides another layer of insulation from the underlying hardware and software application. Technically, an organization could choose to unload the database from one platform and move it to another. The Process Scheduler enables it to migrate all of the offline execution parameters and schedules automatically. Its integration with the online system provides end users with an unprecedented level of control of their reports and offline update processes.

2.4 Data management

Each organization must manage its own data. In fact, data integrity has long been the chief responsibility of central information systems departments. Data adminstrators and programmers must have a means to import and export data, archive data, and manipulate sets of data. Every database format has its own tools and procedures for this. PeopleSoft is no exception. PeopleTools includes three separate tools for data management. Import Manager, Data Mover, and Mass Change each has its own capabilities, and data administrators will likely use them all at different times.

2.4.1 Import Manager

Import Manager is one of the original PeopleTools. As its name suggests, it is designed to import data from sequential data sets into a single table in a PeopleSoft database. All but the lowest-end relational database management systems have their own import utility, but PeopleSoft's has one important distinction, which is especially useful during data conversion. Before Import Manager writes a row to a table, it first checks it for Data Designer edits and processes it through certain types of PeopleCode. This is particularly valuable during data conversion.

During implementation, business decisions will dictate how the organization's data must look. Lookup table edits will differ drastically from the old system, and PeopleCode edits and processing will hide some data validation requirements. Import Manager produces edit reports and rejects rows that fail some or all of the edits, helping developers identify data conversion problems and evaluate the complexity of the conversion. Import Manager is probably not a tool that most organizations will use for any purpose other than data conversion. Since most implementations are phased in, it does get some ongoing use, but for production systems it is not capable enough for most data-moving functions.

2.4.2 Data Mover

Data Mover is a tool suitable for database administrators and programmers to manipulate the database. With it they create, edit, and run scripts that execute SQL statements against the database. It cannot completely replace the tools included with the relational database management system, but it will replace many. The functions of Data Mover are as follows.

- It is a platform-independent means to execute SQL statements against a PeopleSoft database.
- It can archive PeopleSoft tables or databases.
- It can move PeopleSoft databases across operating systems, database platforms, and hardware platforms.

The Data Mover command set consists of SQL commands and Data Mover commands. SQL commands are native SQL statements that run against the database. All SQL commands that require only SQL PREPARE and EXECUTE can be run from Data Mover. It does not, however, support SELECT statements, since they require SQL FETCH operations. (See Table 2.4.)

Table 2.4 SQL and Data Mover Commands

Type	SQL Commands	Data Mover Commands
Commit Processing	COMMIT, ROLLBACK	SET COMMIT, SET NO COMMIT
Data Retrieval		EXPORT
DDL (Data Definition)	CREATE, ALTER, DROP, GRANT	IMPORT, REPLACE_ALL, REPLACE_VIEW, GRANT_USER
DDL		RENAME
DML (Data Manipulation)	INSERT	IMPORT, REPLACE_DATA, REPLACE_ALL
DML	UPDATE, UPDATE	

For organizations using multiple RDBMS platforms, Data Mover offers a single tool to use across all platforms. Scripts used to manipulate database objects on one platform will run against databases on another platform, which simplifies the DBA's job of managing these data manipulation language statements.

Data Mover's Export and Import statements are useful for two functions. First, with Export, individual PeopleSoft tables or entire databases can be extracted and archived in a format that can be reloaded if necessary. Second, developers can move data—including PeopleTools objects such as records and panels—from one database to another and across platforms. Data Mover also provides capabilities to manipulate certain PeopleSoft-specific data types. The STORE and ERASE commands add and remove stored COBOL SQL statements from the stored statements table in PeopleTools. The GRANT and ENCRYPT commands are used to manipulate users and passwords for a PeopleSoft database. Although it is a younger tool, Data Mover is certain to see significant use, especially during installation and upgrades.

2.4.3 Mass Change

Mass Change is a set-processing tool—that is, it manipulates a set of rows in the database that correspond to one or more related tables. It can also be used to archive data, to copy rows of data from one table to another, and to perform common transactions that are not supported using the PeopleSoft panels. Its design consists of three levels. Defining and combining Mass Change properties at these three levels results in a single Mass Change, which can be used to update sets of data. Each level is a conceptual panel group, where developers and/or end users enter appropriate information. Mass Change uses lookup tables and heeds table relationships to limit the types of updates generated to those that follow the logical model of the data in the database.

The lowest level, Mass Change Types, is used by developers to define the underlying SQL statements. Types defines the number of SQL statements that will execute, the order in which they will execute, which rows of data will be affected, and how those rows will be modified. Developers have the option of entering free-form SQL with Mass Change Types, but that is strongly discouraged due to maintenance concerns.

The next level, Mass Change Templates, is built using a specific Mass Change Type as the foundation. A Mass Change Template defines the fields in the SQL statements where the user will be allowed to set criteria. It provides a means whereby extremely restricted selectivity is given to the end user in terms of which records will be manipulated and how they will be changed.

The highest level, Mass Change Definition, is used by end users to actually define a Mass Change they will execute. End users creating new definitions will find that once they select a Mass Change Template, all the information defaults from the template except for selection criteria and default values. Once defined, they can be executed either online, upon saving the panel, or in background via the Process Scheduler.

Combined, these three levels offer developers and end users a good deal of flexibility to define and execute updates against the database. Mass Change is not a tool to replace the typical batch processing, however. It simply fills a niche that neither batch nor online fills particularly well. That niche can be loosely defined as "panelless, user-defined updates to specific rows of data in particular tables." It is a kind of end user ad hoc updating tool. As such, it is extremely powerful, and organizations must ensure that it is tightly controlled. This power carries with it the potential for disaster, and only knowledgeable, accountable staff should be given access to define and use Mass Change.

2.5 PeopleSoft trees

Software systems typically store information or data in files or relational database tables. These data are added, changed, and deleted online by manipulating them with screens. Offline, they are updated by merging other information and business logic with these data using a batch program such as one written in COBOL or C. This is sufficient for most of the data stored by organizations. The relationships between the different types of data are reflected in the structure of the database. A general ledger journal entry, for example, might consist of two types of data: the header information, which applies to all of the lines in the journal entry, and the detail lines, which make up the individual accounting entries. Further, the detail lines will contain information about the account and department (and probably other chart field attributes), which must be checked for valid values.

Table 2.5 Journal_Header and Journal_Line Record Format

Journal_Header Record	Journal_Line Record
JOURNAL_DATE*	JOURNAL_DATE*
JOURNAL_DESCRIPTION	JOURNAL_LINE_NO*
JOURNAL_ID*	JOURNAL_ID*
JOURNAL_TOTAL_CREDITS	DEPT_ID
JOURNAL_TOTAL_DEBITS	ACCOUNT
	JOURNAL_AMOUNT
	JOURNAL_LINE_DESCRIPTION

* Denotes fields that make up the key.

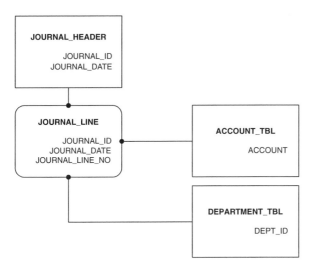

Figure 2.14 Logical relationship between tables

Suppose we have the JOURNAL_HEADER and JOURNAL_LINE tables with the format shown in Table 2.5. The relationships between these two tables and between the the JOURNAL_LINE table and the ACCOUNT and DEPARTMENT tables can be easily diagrammed. Note that the solid black dots on the connector lines connecting the tables represent the many sides of a one-to-many relationship between the tables. (See Figure 2.14.)

We see that the relationship between the tables is discernible in the design of the database. Suppose, however, that we have a single table containing data that, within itself, has this kind of relationship—for example, suppose we have a table that stores all of our valid accounts, their account type, and description. The relationship of the data contained in that table might be similar to that shown in Figure 2.15.

We can write a report to print the contents of the table, but that will not show any relationships between the values. In fact, this relationship is not evident to anyone just by looking at the table and the database structure. We might be able to manage this if we have only a few accounts, but suppose we have hundreds or even thousands of accounts. Maintaining and processing against this relationship becomes unwieldy. It is for this reason that PeopleTools includes the Tree Manager. Tree Manager provides a graphical, point-and-click tool for visually arranging the rows of data into logical hierarchies. Organizations can use the Tree Manager to define types of trees specific to their business or industry.

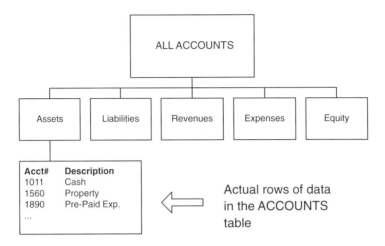

Figure 2.15 Relationship of data in an Accounts Table

PeopleSoft ships three different types of trees. Financial trees, Human Resources trees, and Query trees are used extensively by PeopleSoft application software. (See Figure 2.16.)

2.5.1 Financial Trees

Financial trees are basically used to define the roll-up structure of an organization's chart field values. As in the Account-table example shown in Figure 2.15, the roll-up structure of the entire chart of accounts can be graphically defined. Each Financial Tree summarizes rules and reporting structures for a given chart field. PeopleSoft Financials uses them to roll up summary ledgers, consolidations, and allocations. PeopleSoft nVision uses these tree structures to define the structure and scope of financial reports. When the relationship between the rows of data in a chart field changes, say a new account is added or a department is moved under a different vice president, end users can simply update the trees. The changes will be automatically reflected in the financial reporting, allocations, and consolidations. The Tree Manager's design allows detail values to be updated from within the tree itself. End users who need to change a value in the Accounts table can do so from within the tree, as opposed to going to the Accounts panel group to do it.

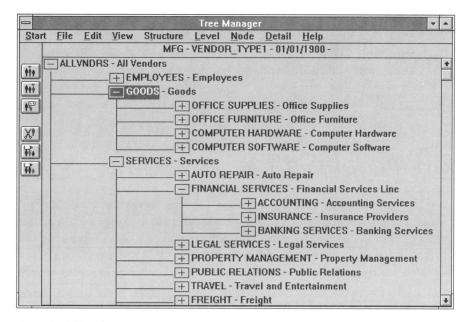

Figure 2.16 Tree Manager screen capture (vendor types)

2.5.2 *Human resources trees*

In its Human Resources system, PeopleSoft uses several types of trees which are worth mentioning here. Organizational Security Trees are based on the organization's hierarchy tree. PeopleSoft uses the departments in this tree to assign security roles for access to the data. Other Human Resources trees include succession planning and position management.

2.5.3 *Query Trees*

PeopleSoft uses trees to define the types of data in the database. Similar tables are grouped together—for example, the Accounts and Departments tables will both be under the chart fields node of the Query Tree. Security access is granted or revoked to these tree nodes, providing a way to manage which users can query which tables. End users can visually locate the tables they wish to query by navigating the Query Tree's descriptive groups to easily locate specific tables.

Trees are a powerful way to represent data in a format that end users can understand. To that end, it meshes well with PeopleSoft's corporate vision. Too many trees, however, soon become a forest, and organizations can find themselves lost in the jungle of tens or hundreds of trees. It is important to carefully plan the number and types of trees an organization will maintain and to ensure that there are reliable processes guaranteeing currency and correctness as the detail data behind the trees evolve over time.

2.6 PeopleSoft security

For much client/server software, security has been a source of concern on the part of central information systems executives and security administrators. Traditional corporate information systems have long been under the watchful and stingy eye of the central security systems owned by most corporations. The chief problem in many organizations is the length of time it can take for a new user to gain access or for an existing user to gain new functionality. Ironically though, security administrators can often revoke access within minutes of the request.

This has probably been a point of contention in organizations, but generally, senior management could sleep soundly at night knowing that their data was relatively safe and secure. New technologies, like the internet, have emerged so rapidly that security packages have been unable to keep up. Client/server is one of these new technologies and is no exception. One of its greatest strengths is also one of the chief reasons that security is so difficult. Client/server software, including PeopleSoft, marries numerous products to manufacture a single, functional system. These differing pieces often have their own, underlying security requirements and often the actual end users are granted more access than security administrators are normally comfortable granting. To see how PeopleSoft implements security, let's examine the specific security tools included with PeopleTools.

2.6.1 Operator Security

Operator Security is a PeopleTool used to permit users to log into the system with a given level of access. With it, administrators define Operator Classes for one or more users with a common set of access. Classes are assigned access to specific menus and, within those menus, specific panels.

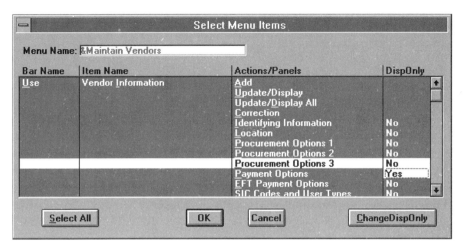

Figure 2.17 Operator Security screen capture (vendor table)

This is an excellent design, because it keeps developers from building hundreds of menus to implement security. If the Maintain Vendors menu contains a panel group of 12 panels, security administrators do not have to give access to all 12 panels to an Operator Class. Suppose a certain class of operators only needs access to the Vendor Address panel and will only display that panel. Using Operator Security, these operators can be granted access to only the Vendor Address panel within the panel group of 12. The "Display/Only" option can be turned on for that panel. That operator class will only see the single Vendor Address panel upon accessing the Maintain Vendors menu. (See Figure 2.17.)

Operator Classes are also assigned valid sign-on times using Operator Security. It controls, by day of the week, between which hours an Operator Class can sign onto the system. It also controls certain Process Scheduler access options, which are assigned at the class level. When Operator Classes are complete, PeopleSoft users are created and assigned to a single Operator Class. This is a serious limitation. Without the capability to assign multiple classes, or "roles," to individual Operator IDs, maintaining them is needlessly complex. Particularly when workflow processing is entered into the mix, the ability to define roles and assign multiple roles to a single user is almost a must. The reality of the workaround is that each user ends up in its own class or users are granted more access than they truly need.

2.6.2 Object Security

Object Security is a completely different security tool for a completely different purpose. Whereas Operator Security controls access to the PeopleSoft applications such as General Ledger and Asset Management, Object Security controls access to the application *development.*

Suppose we want to restrict certain PeopleTools developers so they will only be able to modify panels and tables associated with Accounts Payable. With Object Security, we could create an Object Group containing access to all of the Accounts Payable panels and records. We would then assign our Accounts Payable developers access to this group only. In this way, we can manage the development of our application and ensure that only appropriate staff are making modifications to our software.

2.6.3 Sign-on security

Now let's examine how security interacts with the sign-on process. When a user first invokes the PeopleTools client executable on the workstation, he or she receives the sign-on screen, which prompts for a database name, platform, operator ID, and password. When the user enters the information, PeopleTools carries out a number of steps to complete the sign-on to the database.

Step 1   Connect to the database via the underlying network and database communication protocols

Step 2   Query the database for the OWNERID of the database. This value is stored in the PSDBOWNER table. Each database of a subsystem or instance has a row in this table. PeopleTools uses the database name entered at sign-on to construct the WHERE clause and retrieve the correct OWNERID.

Step 3   The OWNERID from step 2 is used to qualify the table PSLOCK to retrieve the owner of the PeopleSoft tables.

Select PSOWNERID from OWNERID.PSLOCK.
This PSOWNERID will be used to qualify the tables in the next step.

Step 4   The system selects a row from the PSOWNERID.PSOPRDEFN table to retrieve a security profile for the ID entered by the user. The system retrieves access ID, access password, and operator password. It compares the operator password with the one entered by the user.

Step 5   If the operator password is valid, the system disconnects from the database and reconnects the access ID and access password, retrieved in step 4, for the user.

This strategy effectively makes each user the owner of the database. So, from a technical level, every client has database authority to manipulate all of the PeopleSoft tables including DROP and CREATE rights. PeopleSoft relies on the the security profile established with Operator Security and Object Security to restrict access.

The positive side of this is that if an end user attempts to sign onto the database independent of PeopleSoft, using native database management tools, his or her operator ID will have only Select authority to the very few security tables outlined in the previous steps. Since PeopleSoft encrypts passwords using the National Security Administrator's DES algorithm, the database is safe from tampering outside of PeopleTools. Only the security adminstrator should know the access ID and password in order to protect this security feature.

2.6.4 Functional security

Security to the software's functionality is established and controlled using the security classes described in Section 2.6.1. By creating classes and assigning menus, panel groups, or partial panel groups and actions to those classes, security adminstrators control which portions of the applications and which actions each end user can invoke.

2.6.5 Row-level and field-level security

Two additional types of security are row- and field-level security. Often, end users need to update information on various panels, but not all potential rows of data on those panels—for instance, organizations may wish to restrict end users from making journal entries using any business units other than their own. This row-level restriction is provided by using security views. PeopleSoft ships several security views for use with its software. They are used as filters during search key entry to restrict the rows that are updated or added to those that are defined in the view for a particular operator ID.

Table 2.6 Security Tools

Security Type	Tools
Application Function Security	Operator Security Classes and Operator IDs
Database Security	Relational Database Management System tools
Field-Level Security	PeopleCode
Network Security	Tools provided by the network operating system
PeopleSoft Sign-on Security	Operator Security and Relational Database Management tools
PeopleTools Object Security	Object Security
Row-Level Security	Data Designer and Security Views

PeopleSoft claims to support field-level security, but that is a little misleading. Field-level security, at its roots, is really hard-coding specific access on each field. What PeopleSoft will sell as field-level security is really no more capable than what is offered by most software vendors. Using PeopleCode, developers can control access to individual fields by using the Hide(fieldname) and Gray(fieldname) functions. This does create field-level security, but it must be maintained by developers as opposed to security administrators. For this reason, it is usually used to restrict access to certain specialized fields by individual operators or classes as a means of controlling them more closely. It is not a wise approach to use field-level security extensively, since it will require significant maintenance over time.

2.6.6 Batch-processing security

Security for offline processing is much trickier than for online processing. PeopleSoft uses third-party software such as Crystal Report Writer, SQR, and COBOL for much of its batch processing, and these software interact with the database independent of PeopleSoft's online security scheme. End users running these batch programs either must have the access ID and password, or database administrators must create their own users, grant appropriate access, and create synonymns of the PeopleSoft tables. The best strategy is to require end users to submit and run batch jobs from within the online system using Process Scheduler. Process Scheduler isolates the value of access passwords from the user by sending it as part of the WinExec statement, which launches the batch program.

Security issues We've seen that security is implemented using more than a single tool (see Table 2.6). It is important for security administrators to clearly define the profiles and maintain them in a logical, understandable format. The array of tools and different options will be a problem when security administrator staff changes, and clearly documented guidelines and profiles will ease the transition.

The addition of network and database security into the mix will further confuse the issue since these are not always administered by the same positions in an organization. The complexity and number of tools and options make it critical for the implementation team to carefully plan the software's security strategy. The team should work closely with security administrators and seek the advice and guidance of PeopleSoft experts to develop and implement that strategy.

2.7 PeopleSoft development steps

To sum up the PeopleTools development environment, let's examine the steps involved in creating a small sample application. Suppose we want to track an inventory of notebook computers available for staff to check out. The system will consist of two database tables, NOTEBOOK and NB_ACTIVITY. It will consist of a single panel to check the computers in and out. It will have two menu items: one to check out and one to check in the computers.

Step1   *Create record definitions* The foundation of the system is its underlying database structure. The first step is to define that structure. We will use the Data Designer to create the following record definitions.

NOTEBOOK	Fields	NB_ACTIVITY	Fields
NB_ID	CHAR(8) key	NB_ID	CHAR(8) key
DESCRIPTION	CHAR(30)	ACTION_DATE	DATE key
CPU_MODEL	CHAR(10)	ACTION	CHAR(1) key
PURCH_DATE	DATE	PERSON	CHAR(5)
		DESCRIPTION	CHAR(30)

In this step we also specify which fields we want to have as search keys, or lookup keys. Fields such as PERSON field and CPU_MODEL would likely have associated prompt and edit tables. We would also specify default values and programming logic in the form of PeopleCode, as well as any additional search views needed to control access to our panels. (See Figure 2.18.)

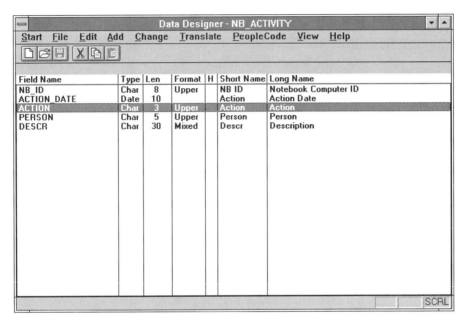

Figure 2.18 NB_ACTIVITY record definition

Step 2   *SQL Create tables and views*   The second step is to create the tables and views using SQL. We have several options to do this. In this case, we generate the SQL CREATE statements for the views and tables in PeopleSoft's Data Mover format. Using Data Mover, we will execute the SQL statements and create the database objects. Typically, this function is performed by a database administrator to enforce organizational data standards.

Step 3   *Create the panel*   Next, we will use the Panel Designer to place fields onto our panel that will be used to update

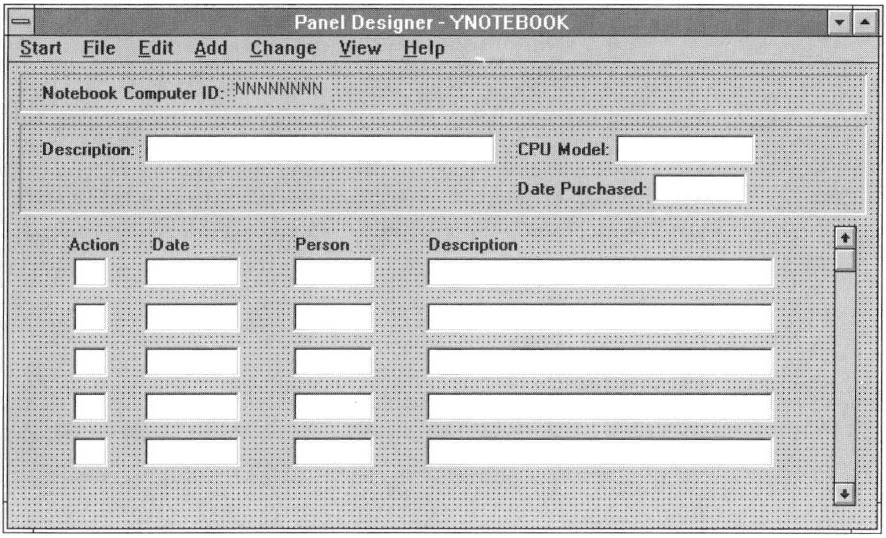

Figure 2.19 Panel definition for Notebook panel

the database. In this case, we'd likely have data from our NOTEBOOK table at the top of the panel and the NB_ACTIVITY within a scroll bar in order to view and add multiple activities at a time for a given computer. (See Figure 2.19.)

Step 4   *Add the panel to a menu* After we have created our records and panel, we are ready to place the panel on a menu. We choose the appropriate menu and add our panel as a panel group. We give it a menu name and description and define a search record. In our case, we'll place our panel on two different menus—each with a different search record. Menu1 will use VIEW1 as its search record, and it will only retrieve records that are available for check out. The menu item will be Check Out Notebook. Menu2 will use VIEW2 and will be called Return Notebooks.

We now have two menu options. Each option invokes our single panel, but will access different types of records. In this way, we built the menu around the process. We might just as easily have created a single menu for both check out and return, but for our users, this is more intuitive.

Step 5   *Set up operator security*   Before any users can access our new panel, we must update their operator profiles. Specifically, we must grant access to the two menu options to each operator class that will access them. At this point, our online modifications are complete.

The steps above outline the process of adding simple, online processes to PeopleSoft applications. An experienced developer could accomplish this task in about an hour, assuming the requirements were gathered previously. At the other end of the spectrum, a complex subsystem of tens of tables complete with complex PeopleCode logic and several panels might take an experienced developer a few days or more to build and test.

Omitted from this discussion are offline processes. Suppose we needed to create an update program to flag notebook computers that need to be scrapped, and we wanted several reports to support the operational procedures associated with the check-out process. These programs would have their associated requirements gathering and design considerations, as well as coding and testing. Often, these offline programs require the most effort to complete.

The process for adding online functionality to PeopleSoft appears to be relatively simple, and that is, in fact, a major strength of PeopleTools. Business experts, not programmers, can use PeopleTools to build applications relatively easily. Its rapid, iterative development cycle facilitates prototyping, and designing can be a cooperative effort between end users and developers. PeopleTools excels at implementing business logic at exceedingly high productivity levels. Once developers master the Data Designer and Panel Designer and have a thorough understanding of the underlying database structure of PeopleSoft application software, PeopleTools allows them to very quickly build and test additional functionality. This is crystal-clear during a demonstration of PeopleSoft, and many may extrapolate this into other areas of development such as analysis and design and batch-process programming, which have productivity levels largely independent of the programming tools used. It is important to remember that offline programs will take much longer to design, code, and test than online programs. All in all, however, PeopleTools is an excellent development platform for building business applications, and many organizations will find it an excellent way to transition to client/server technology.

chapter 3

Expertise

One common thread running through all organizations moving from traditional software to client/server is the importance of training. The corporate world glaringly lacks professionals who possess the skills, expertise, and experience to transform the technological infrastructures of their organizations. PeopleSoft clients are no exception. Those who are fortunate enough to have anyone this capable will still find themselves with a project team that is woefully ill-equipped to deal with the complexities involved in the implementation. Organizations must invest the time and money to develop the necessary skills in the project team and to propagate this expertise throughout the organization when and where it is appropriate. PeopleSoft is technically complex, integrating layer upon layer of software—all of which must work in harmony. The Financials applications are also feature-rich, and therefore complicated to master. The implementation will bring database administrators and network support staff together for perhaps the first time, and it will be a new experience for both. System performance tuning will be exponentially more difficult than in a traditional software system due to this conglomeration of technologies. PeopleSoft Financials will beg for new levels of business expertise in the technical staff and technical expertise in the end user staff. Acquiring this expertise and pushing it out to the organization is critical to guarantee the success of the project. The eventual survival of the project team depends also on how executive management is involved in the implementation. Because the implementation will require an immense training investment to be successful, project managers should possess a solid understanding of what types of training are needed— when and by whom. They can use this information to prepare and justify training plans to accompany the project plan.

3.1 Technical complexity of PeopleSoft

To demonstrate the complex nature of PeopleSoft Financials, let's examine the layers involved in generating a report and contrast them with those found in traditional systems.

3.1.1 Traditional software

In a traditional, mainframe-based system, generating a report typically involves running a program, which reads the data from the database and sends these data to the mainframe print queue specified in the job control statements. In its most complex form, a report program communicates with a database manager and sends data to a print queue, which

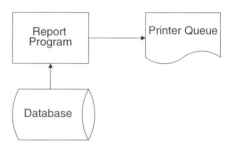

Figure 3.1 Software layers of a mainframe report

is controlled at the operating system level and probably involves some communication component. (See Figure 3.1.)

3.1.2 PeopleSoft Financials

Comparing the relative simplicity of the mainframe system with People-Soft will illuminate precisely why it is technically difficult to master. To

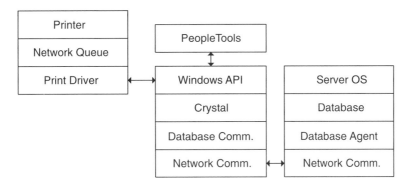

Figure 3.2 Software layers of a PeopleSoft report

generate a report, an end user must access a report menu from the appropriate application window and submit the report request via the Run button on the PeopleSoft toolbar. PeopleCode will execute to call a Microsoft Windows function to start a new task, Crystal Reports. The program will pass the report name and other associated parameters to Crystal. Crystal will start, accessing the appropriate report, and retrieve the data from the database. To do this, Crystal must "talk" to a database API, which in turn talks to a network API, which is translated to network messages to the database server. At the database server, the network messages communicate to a particular database listening agent, which passes the query to the database for processing. For the data to return to Crystal, the same path is required. Once Crystal has its data, it formats the information based on the report layout and sends it to the currently defined printer, most likely a network printer queue, which introduces another layer of communication. This description is a simplification; reality may show 12 or more individual layers of software from various vendors communicating in harmony to generate the report. (See Figure 3.2.)

3.2 Essential technical skills

3.2.1 Workstation

To begin our discussion about training requirements, we'll start, logically, at the client side of the client/server software. The most obvious software skill essential for all PeopleSoft users is Microsoft Windows. Each member of the project team must be proficient at Microsoft Windows. Technical staff will also need to be adept at working in the Windows environment. End users must master some advanced capabilities of the operating system in order to take full advantage of PeopleSoft. The more casual user will need less understanding, but many organizations may be moving from Windows 3.1 to one of the 32-bit options and this will require some retraining for all users.

The PeopleSoft user who is responsible only for accessing the software, performing some process such as purchase order entry, and generating some basic reports will need to be a capable Windows operator. These users should understand the concept of opening and closing windows on the desktop and should know the difference between closing a window and minimizing a window. Each time a user accesses a PeopleSoft window from the Start menu, the software invokes a new copy of that window and minimizes the invoking window. Novice users might complain that, after awhile, their workstation slows to a crawl, has frequent system errors, and hangs completely. Often, support staff will examine the workstation during one of these problem periods and find that the user has 15 or more open PeopleSoft windows, many of which are duplicated. This might be in addition to several resource-intensive programs such as word processing and spreadsheet software. Good Microsoft Windows operation and management skills are essential.

The power users, those who will heavily use the software and will create and generate a significant number of reports, will need more Microsoft Windows expertise. Specifically, these users need to understand how multiple applications work together. Cut-and-paste operations—switching between active programs and sharing data between programs using dynamic data exchange or object linking and embedding—are required to fully utilize the entire software suite. Advanced tools such as nVision and Query can work with and through other applications to create reports with graphics, links to other databases, mail-merge reports, and so on. It will be the power users who will define the advanced functions on which the organization will come to rely. Users without a good understanding of the advanced capabilities will likely fall short of providing the optimum solution.

Technical staff will be asked to manipulate their Microsoft Windows environment on a daily basis. Developers will often work with multiple versions of PeopleSoft software throughout a given time period, and they will need to set the operating environment to support this. PeopleSoft provides a template process to manage this, but each site will need to modify it to fit their computing infrastructure. They must be proficient at INI file management, setting environment variables, modifying the path, and installing and upgrading Windows-based applications. In short, they really should be conceptual "systems programmers" for their individual workstation in order to achieve the highest level of productivity.

3.2.2 *PeopleSoft technical skills*

The degree to which implementation team members and end users will need to know and understand the PeopleSoft application and the development tools depends on the implementation strategy, level of end user responsibility, and the degree of involvement of each individual. Developers will need some knowledge of the application's functionality, and the end users on the implementation team will need to have some knowledge of the workings of PeopleTools. The training overlap should lean to the side of the team that is driving the implementation—for example, if the project leadership and ultimate responsibility lie with the developers, they should attend as much end user training on the application itself as the end users. Conversely, if the project leader is an end user, that person at a minimum needs a solid foundation on the workings of PeopleTools. To successfully prototype, the participants will need a combination of application knowledge and PeopleTools skills. The degree to which the project leader can blend both skills will determine the productivity of the sessions and will affect the dynamics of the implementation.

Each team member should know how the application functions globally. Specific departments will have to learn functions that support their operations in much greater detail. Everyone ought to understand how accounting information flows from the various modules into general ledger, but only the accounts payable staff, for example, need to concern themselves with check-sorting options. Developers will probably not have the luxury of detailed knowledge of the modules, but they will need to concentrate on the parts of the software they'll be customizing. However, it will be invaluable, for all who are able, to study the application data models provided by PeopleSoft in order to gain an understanding of the tables, fields, and their relationships. It's an excellent way to grasp the scope of the application without learning all of the panels and processes. Application expertise requirements are really determined dynamically, by the team itself. The guideline is basically to ensure that everyone has enough knowledge to make informed decisions in their circles of influence or control.

Development tool skills are a little more emotional. Particularly if an organization's information system is still fairly centralized, it can be an area of disagreement. In truth, all members of the working implementation team should have basic PeopleTools training. At the very least, they should be confident creating a record definition and creating a simple panel. Team members with greater responsibility will need even more technical training, and the developers should have as much as the organization can be coaxed into buying. PeopleSoft training courses are hands-on, lab-oriented courses, which are very good by industry standards. Unlike some training sessions, attendees will return full of information, questions, cheat-sheets, and ideas. It is a good idea to estimate the amount of training the project team will need before signing a contract with PeopleSoft, in order to bargain for additional training units to be included with the software. Purchasing additional units is expensive and a little forethought here can save organizations thousands of dollars.

3.2.3 Database administration and network skills

Moving from a traditional, mainframe-based financial system to client/server may or may not be an organization's first experience with relational database management systems, but it is almost certain to be the first time that the network and database are so intertwined. Client/server software can present new challenges to the network support staff and to database administrators.

To begin with, PeopleSoft Financials is made up of literally hundreds of tables in a single database. Some of the tables are extremely volatile, while others remain static almost indefinitely. PeopleSoft also includes a large number of indexes, some of which are appropriate while others are either inefficient or unused. Database administrators must have the expertise and the perseverance to tune the database to fit the organization. Because the application is so large, it requires a significant effort to appropriately size and manage the database. The database administrators assigned to the project must be experienced with the relational database management system. They must be schooled in proper database management techniques to guarantee the accuracy and stability of the data for the organization. It would be a major blunder to assign a novice, and it may be necessary to recruit and hire someone with the appropriate skills to safeguard against catastrophe.

The integration of the database with the client requires appropriate networking software and hardware, which in turn requires network personnel. Typically, most organizations implementing PeopleSoft will have existing network staff and an infrastructure on which the software will run. The organization's network staff needs a solid understanding of network design, performance tuning, and monitoring and should be able to work closely with the database administrators and developers to assist in troubleshooting and performance tuning. As long as the network staff is proactive in its approach to increasing the organization's network, and it possesses the requisite people skills to enable collaboration with the development and database staff, the project will have few network problems that cannot readily be solved.

3.2.4 Performance tuning

Performance tuning can be one of the functions overlooked in the formal project planning process. Without it, the application will not perform acceptably in all areas. Client/server runs inherently slower than traditional, transaction-processing software, and certain portions will not perform acceptably as delivered. In order to tune them, developers, database administrators, and network specialists must join forces and go beyond the typical performance tuning processes. The group must be able to analyze the performance of workstation software, network operating systems, the network itself, SQL statements, the database management system, and the server hardware and software. Since performance problems in any of these areas can manifest themselves as a slow-performing PeopleSoft application, the organization must ensure that technical staff has these skills. They are best developed over time, but the staff must understand all of the components and how they interact with one another in order to begin building these skills as the needs arise.

3.2.5 Business acumen

The entire decision to endure the trauma and expense of implementing PeopleSoft Financials can be justified in business terms. More than likely, the organization's existing financial software is not meeting the needs of today's business climate, and end users are demanding more responsive and better-functioning software with more useful information. The implementation team needs to understand and appreciate these business concerns. Business process reengineering skills are critical to make sure the new software functions effectively for the organization. Gone are the days when end users requested a system from central information systems, which in turn went off for two years and then returned with its idea of their requirements. PeopleSoft is software *of the people,* and those people do not speak technical jargon. It is incumbent upon the technical staff to meet the end users on their turf. Technical staffers who do not understand concepts such as business processes and cost/benefit analysis are really a liability to the implementation project. In the PeopleSoft paradigm, developers must see themselves as process facilitators and business problem solvers rather than technical gurus. The search for technical nirvana has killed many software implementation projects, and no application is more susceptible to this than PeopleSoft financials. It is probably easier to hire functional financial experts and teach them the technical skills than to teach technically focused computer professionals the essential business skills. The good news is that many of today's software developers can bridge this gap. Organizations where this is not the case will need to secure this expertise before attempting the implementation.

3.2.6 Adaptability

It is apparent that to successfully implement PeopleSoft, organizations must have access to the upper echelon of software implementation personnel. The project will be difficult to manage. The relationships between technical staff, end users, support personnel, and senior management must be taken into account. The project will change considerably as it passes through its various stages and it will demand much of the staff assigned to it. These people, to succeed with their sanity intact, must absorb change rapidly, learn more quickly than most, and adapt to the changing needs of the project. They must feel more like a SWAT team than a typical software development team. The software and the project will provide enough motivation, as long as the people involved possess these skills, for the team to be responsive and productive. Without them, however, the project is likely to drag on as old techniques are erroneously applied.

3.3 How to arm the organization with the essential skills

In order to standardize an organization on the PeopleSoft financials software suite, the organization must first commit to Microsoft Windows as the desktop operating system. This is not as mindless a decision as it might seem, because Windows comes in three flavors—each with its own strengths and weaknesses. Windows 3.1, Windows 95, and Windows NT Workstation are all different forms of the Microsft Windows family of operating environments under which PeopleSoft can run. Most organizations will standardize on one of these as their desktop operating systems. Once that decision is made, then the organization can begin to prepare the staff to be able to effectively use PeopleSoft Financials.

Experience is an excellent teacher, and with a desktop operating system, it is critical for users to feel confident with its major features. Usually, some members of the technical staff in the organization will be experts at Windows simply from heavy use and from supporting the distribution of Windows throughout the corporation. If this is not the case, then the organization must select an appropriate individual to undergo exhaustive education on the appropriate Windows environment. This individual should team up with the professional development personnel and develop a systematic training program for all PeopleSoft users. For the training to be successful, each participant should have his or her own workstation, and the curriculum should weigh heavily toward lab excercises. It is also important for the participants to return to their jobs and apply what they've learned; otherwise, they will soon forget and the organization will have wasted time and money. A caveat about workstation training: Be sure it is not too technical. Users should understand how to apply the features of the operating system and, in particular, how they apply to PeopleSoft. Anything more will confuse and frustrate the novice user and waste the time of the more capable user.

3.3.1 Acquiring PeopleSoft expertise

Of all the expenses involved in implementing PeopleSoft Financials, the most costly is going to be gaining the experience and knowledge required for successful implementation. This cannot be stressed enough. There is no single issue more critical to the project than that of training. A well-trained implementation team and users who are competent in the software's functionality are the springboard for the entire project. How individual members develop this expertise depends on their roles in the organization and on the project team.

In general, there are three ways to gain PeopleSoft expertise. The fastest way is to hire someone who has experience with PeopleSoft Financials. This is probably a preferred method, but it is extremely difficult and expensive. The market for PeopleSoft's customers base continues to grow so fast that the industry cannot turn out enough experts to keep up. In fact, most experienced professionals fend off a constant barrage of headhunters trying to woo them away from their current positions to place them with other, new PeopleSoft customers. These people are some of the highest-paid professionals in the industry, and it will take more than just money to entice them to make a change. Plan to offer them high salary, a choice position, excellent benefits, and a good working environment. With the right offer, an appropriate person may simply be plugged in as the PeopleSoft expert from the outset of the project. This is an ideal situation, and if the organization can afford to, it should explore this option from the outset.

The second way to gain the expertise is to send the staff to training. PeopleSoft provides a comprehensive training program ranging from the PeopleTools technical courses to detailed functional ones. It is crucial to provide intense training for the project team at the very beginning of the implementation. The technical staff must attend PeopleTools courses, PeopleCode courses, and SQR programming, as well as system administration and upgrade. All project team members will ideally attend application training such as General Ledger or Accounts Payable. With the project team all on the same page as far as knowledge of the software, they can better evaluate the fit of the package and the impact of various customizations. If the organization cannot afford to provide that training to the technical team members, the technical leader should at least be included in this.

The training provided by PeopleSoft is thorough and hands-on. Participants will find that they are exposed to far more of the system than they will likely use during the first phases of the installation. They will have questions and ideas upon returning home, and the demonstration databases created during the PeopleSoft installation process need to be available for their use. Any time wasted between attending training and actually making use of the new information results in a loss of retention.

If possible, after training, organizations should set aside time for the participants during the subsequent weeks to solidify their understanding and apply what they've learned. The breadth and depth of the team's knowledge directly affects the quality and speed of the implementation. The training's expense and its importance to the project justify this additional time by maximizing the training dollars' return on investment. Organizations will find training expenditures reasonably close to the same level as those for the software itself, and mishandling the process is a very expensive mistake. (See Table 3.1.)

A typical scenario for software training is for a firm to send a programmer to three courses on the technical People-Tools topics. So, the programmer attends PeopleTools I, PeopleTools II, and PeopleCode training, returns to work, and is immediately thrown into three weeks of current process modeling. With no time to solidify what he or she learned, the pro-

Table 3.1 Sample cost for a single, four-day course at a PeopleSoft Training Center

Expense Category	Amount
Training units charges	$2,000
Travel	$350
Lodging	$600
Food	$150
Miscellaneous	$100
Total for a single course for one person	$3,200

grammer, for a total of $9,600, is left with only a foggy idea of how PeopleTools functions. If, instead, the programmer returned to two weeks of training reiteration time, after five weeks and $9,600, the programmer would be a proficient PeopleTools developer. The difference is the additional two weeks. Plan to build this time into the organization's training schedule and implementation timeline, in order to maximize return on investment.

Most of the other technical skills required for the implementation should be readily available from the organization's infrastructure. It won't hurt, however, to ensure that the individuals who possess the network and database administration skills are identified and officially allocated to the project. The specific skills necessary for PeopleSoft implementation will be acquired during the installation process, but it is a good idea for network and database staff to prepare in advance by scanning the installation documentation from PeopleSoft.

3.3.2 The legacy programmer

The legacy programmer is a sensitive subject, which most organizations must address at some level when they make the decision to move to client/server technology. To help us understand what it means to be a legacy programmer, we must discuss who they are and how they came to be.

In the very early days of computing, large organizations bought mainframe computers to crunch numbers and improve some of their manual transaction processing, which supported their operations. During the 1960s and 1970s, these computers proliferated the corporate and public sector worlds at a rapid rate. In order to make use of these computers, organizations had to find people to write the programs to support their business needs. Unfortunately, formal educational institutions could not produce enough qualified individuals to meet the demand, so organizations were forced to train their own programmers in-house. People who were not trained in computer science or in engineering principles were basically given a few manuals and told to computerize some manual process. These early programmers were bold enough and creative enough to figure out how to accomplish these tasks, so off they went into their mysterious computer world, returning on white horses with "computerized" procedures. In many ways, they were heroes and pioneers in the industry. They deserve much credit for their contributions, but they had many more limitations than today's programmers.

First and foremost, the computer software industry was born literally overnight. First came machine language; then assemblers, which were much easier to learn; and eventually language compilers were developed for various purposes. These early programmers had no access to fundamentals of software engineering principles. They coded their programs using the constraints of assembler coding and, indeed, many of them learned to program using only that low-level programming language. These people literally learned as they went. Quite truthfully, not all of them were good choices to break this new ground and develop good programming practices from nothing but their own vision of software development methodologies. Many of them, by today's standards, would show little aptitude for software development and would not be in the computing workforce.

As the mystique of computers and computer programmers grew, it became fashionable to write "cool" programs. Programs that did tricky, never-before-used processing were often the ones programmers were most proud of. These programs were horrendous to maintain, so offered a degree of job security. This problem was exacerbated by the limitations of the hardware itself. These early computers had little direct access storage capacity and almost no real memory storage by today's standards. As a result, programmers used creative ways to minimize the resources needed by their programs. Efficiency was the highest priority at the expense of maintainability or portability. Data input records were limited by the 80-position size of the punch-card machine, and programmers were frequently required to represent data with fewer positions than they needed. It was common to find that the date was stored using only five digits: two for the month, two for the day, and one for the year—with the century digit being hard-coded in the programs themselves as opposed to being stored with the data. Never mind whether the programs could survive the turn of the century—they could not survive the turn of the decade without maintenance.

Now, many of these programmers came to be COBOL programmers, because their organizations heard from IBM or from some seminar that COBOL was a language that business people could use. It was "English-like." It was going to dramatically improve productivity, so they should immediately move their organizations to this new language. Assembler programmers were handed the COBOL manual and, in traditional fashion, told they would now use it. So they did just that. They coded their programs the same way they would have coded them in assembler, only they used COBOL verbs, creating unbelievably convoluted programs filled with confusing GO TO logic and terrible design. In fact, much of COBOL's poor reputation is directly attributable to pathetic coding practices and habits of the early days. Today, COBOL is a very useful and often most appropriate programming language for offline, file-processing programs common in business applications; however, younger information systems professionals consider it to be a second-class citizen—behind C and C++.

As organizations grew and their informations systems departments expanded, they inevitably got better at software engineering principles and methods. Most people coming into the industry today are armed with basic software engineering methods and are committed to reuse, maintainability, and portability. However, many of the legacy programmers have been left behind. They are still maintaining old systems and are not trained in new tools and techniques. It is quite likely that PeopleSoft Financials will replace some of this legacy code and that these programmers won't have the skills to contribute. It is imperative that the organzations plan for this eventuality and establish a transition path for these individuals.

In the best of worlds, these programmers will be ready, willing, and able to jump right into the new technological world of client/server with all its uncertainties and demand for discipline. But it is not a perfect world, and the reality is that some may not be able to make the transition. Event-driven programming found in client/server software is a distinct paradigm; it is different from traditional programs, which start at the first line of code and proceed until reaching a STOP RUN statement. Some legacy programmers may find this change too difficult to master at this stage in their careers. Some may not have the desire and will seek to transfer or retire. At any rate, it is not good project management to assign tasks to people who are not both competent and confident in the skills required to complete them. It is simply not playing the odds. In order to ensure success, the project manager must eliminate as many fail points as possible and then defuse those that remain. Undercapable staff is a fail point that must be eliminated; therefore, organizations need to evaluate these legacy programmers to make sure they are utilized appropriately. It is a good idea to assign them some tasks to gauge their aptitude before assigning them to a PeopleSoft implementation. A small Visual Basic program, which accepts data from a screen, edits it, and stores it in a relational table, will test their ability to learn SQL, graphical screen design, and event-driven processing. A two-week stint is plenty. After the task is either completed or cancelled, the programmer's supervisor and the programmer must together sit down and evaluate the process. They must focus on how comfortable the programmer feels about the new techniques and whether he or she is excited about them or terrified by the prospect of being held accountable for productively using them. Management, from the beginning, must be completely honest with them and what their options will be. If the programming job has changed that radically, then the programmer needs to know it, so he or she can decide if it is time to commit to retraining or to find a different line of work. In realilty, the decision may not be as clear-cut as one would think, and those who stay will each have a different learning curve and rate. The project tasks vary enough to accommodate these different levels, and managers must match them carefully to the appropriate staff member. (See Table 3.2.)

Table 3.2 Project tasks and descriptions

Task	Description
System Design	System design requires the most skilled developers. They may not be the fastest coders, but they must possess a solid understanding of relational database modeling and of graphical design and event-driven programming. With PeopleSoft, there will not be a massive amount of system design, since the organization is purchasing the design with the software, but extensions to the system must be designed appropriately if they are to fit with the PeopleSoft base system.
Online Panel Programming	Coding the online, graphical user interface programs is a little less demanding than system design, assuming the designer lays out the panels' organization for the coder. If not, then the coders must be able to use good user-interface techniques to avoid building panels which are clumsy for the end user. These programmers must fully understand event-driven programming and must also be able to understand and apply the software's data model appropriately.
Batch Programming	Batch or offline programs are a little less demanding and are good candidates to assign to legacy programmers who are assimilating the new technologies more slowly than others. They will have to learn a new programming language, SQR, since that is PeopleSoft's batch language of choice for all but the most critical programs. The most critical skill for these programs is SQL. Poor SQL can result in poor-performing programs or those that are difficult to maintain. Given that legacy programmers are used to navigating their own databases, they will be less likely to take advantage of relational views and complex table joins to minimize the processing in their programs. Project managers need to be aware of this so as to gently prod them to apply these advantages of the SQL syntax. It is also an opportunity to teach them about SQL tuning. With proper guidance, most programmers can quickly become proficient batch SQR coders, providing they receive up-front SQL training and are given appropriate guidance along the way.

Legacy programmers who can attain proficiency in the PeopleSoft technical skills are an invaluable resource for organizations. Their knowledge of the old software is not shared by all members of the project team, and they can be a major force in the data conversion efforts. In fact, that may be the best way to take advantage of their knowledge and to transition them into PeopleSoft. As data conversion unfolds, they'll have to learn SQL, SQR programming, and the design of the PeopleSoft database. That is an excellent foundation on which to add the PeopleTools training program in order to develop a complete and valuable client/server developer. Again, not all will be able to make this transition, and organizations need to find some mutually beneficial means of moving those who cannot or will not adapt. For those who successfully transform their skills, it is an excellent opportunity for them to receive intensive training and experience to become skilled in the latest and greatest. It must be marketed that way, and those who make the effort and are successful should be rewarded with compensation, choice assignments, or both.

3.4 Functional expertise on the implementation team

Installing a new, complex software package purchased from a vendor is unbelievably difficult. The major stumbling block is that nobody in the organization understands the inner workings of the package. With in-house software, developers have design documentation (at least they should have) and business requirements and the background of why processes work as they do. Knowledge of PeopleSoft will exist nowhere in the organization. The problem is intensified because much of the software's capability will never be used and gets in the way when analyzing its fit with the organization. For this reason, it is essential that the implementation team factor functional knowledge into the training plans. The team must address PeopleSoft functional knowledge on the implementation team—both technical and functional staff—and organization-specific process understanding of the end users on the team. (See Figure 3.3.)

The technical staff will have the most difficulty comprehending the functionality match between the software and the organization. They might know how the old system works, but are less likely to know why it works a particular way and in which areas it falls short. The implementation team will look to them, however, to bridge the gap between the PeopleSoft technology and the application functionality. How to fill the requirements in quadrant C of Figure 3.3 is the responsibility of the technical staff. In order to do this, they must know how the system operates. Indeed, even to test their own customizations, they must know how data flow through the system and what major processes are involved. For this reason, all technical staff on the implementation team should attend

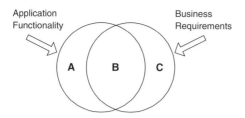

A represents functionality not needed by the organization
B represents where the application meets the organization's needs.
C represents where the application falls short of the organization's needs.

To accurately superimpose the application functionality onto the organization's requirements, software expertise and organizational knowledge are blended in a matrix and areas A, B and C are defined.

Figure 3.3 Application functionality and business requirements

the functional training. If an organization is implementing general ledger, accounts payable, and purchasing, the programmers and project leader on the team must attend those courses as well as the technical PeopleTools courses. They will not have the broad understanding of the end users (they are not financial professionals; they are information systems professionals) but they will be able to understand how the system works and where to go to look for specific functions. Without this training, the technical staff will depend too heavily on the team's end users, reducing the productivity of everyone.

Another key area of expertise required is that of functional knowledge of the organization. Each organization has its own business rules and historical reasons for its various processes. The implementation team must have this knowledge in order to evaluate the various alternatives available in each decision. The only way to make sure this knowledge is available is to assign those with the expertise to either serve on the implementation team or to be available whenever needed. It is possible to implement without this expertise, but the chance of politically devastating errors increases dramatically.

The pivotal area of expertise, however, is that the end users on the implementation team understand the functionality of the application. The accounts payable staff involved in the implementation must truly understand how the PeopleSoft Accounts Payable application functions, what it does well, what it does poorly, and what it does not do at all. They cannot rely on the technical team members to provide this perspective.

With the scope of the software, organizations can easily overlook the specifics of a particular process—only to get burned when they cut over to production. One organization assumed that the accounts payable staff handled discounts earned and lost in a manner that was consistent with its past practices. Their departments were used to realizing the discounts earned and "eating" those that were lost. It was not until the night before going live that the implementation team recognized it would have to introduce a new process into the system to maintain the current business practice. Had the users really understood the Accounts Payable interface to the General Ledger, this quandary would have been eliminated from the beginning.

In many organizations, the end user departments are organized and staffed more to shuffle paper and carry out manual processes, as opposed to the PeopleSoft paradigm of informed decision-making and exception processing. This can be a problem when those people are not properly educated and/or trained to take on the new roles. Former data entry operators may find themselves managing procurement contracts or holding payments for vendors because they are not meeting quality levels. It is critical that these people attend the formal PeopleSoft training and that the demonstration databases provided be available upon their return. They must also be willing and able to share what they learn with others in their areas in order to spread the expertise around. To fully leverage PeopleSoft's advantages, the end users must be able to apply a broad range of its functionality. This can only be accomplished when they understand how it works.

The implementation team will never cut over to production with total perfection. They will surely miss some requirements and scramble for a few weeks after going live to tidy up the software before moving on. The key is to minimize the number and scope of these "package holes" by arming the team with the appropriate functional expertise.

3.5 The rest of the organization

Apart from the intensive training required by the implementation team, other individuals throughout the organization will require some degree of training or exposure to the PeopleSoft software. The degree of training and the number involved is really only determined after the scope of the project is known. The degree to which the software is pushed out into the various departments dictates who will need training and in what form they will need it. To help us understand the different types of training that are needed, we will examine various organizational roles and how to train the people in them.

3.5.1 Power users

Power users are those who use the application extensively. These people will depend on the PeopleSoft Financials modules to carry out their daily jobs. They will use a broad range of the software's functionality and will be responsible for preparing reports on some level. These people should attend the formal application training provided by PeopleSoft if at all possible. The number of power users in an organization will vary with its size, but it is a relatively small number at any rate. With the broad understanding gained from the course work, these users have a context in which to help expand the software with the organization. An untrained power user may apply the software in nonoptimal ways due to a lack of understanding of the assumptions and design inherent in PeopleSoft. Often, misapplication of the software snowballs into quirky offline processing logic and tedious, counterproductive reporting requirements. For that reason, those people should attend the formal training whenever possible, and they should be encouraged to continue learning the software as it evolves. The question of whom to send to which training courses requires careful consideration by the implementation team. Certain power users may need training in multiple applications, depending upon their level of cross-functional integration. Accounts payable and purchasing staff may need to overlap some training to gain a solid understanding of the integration between the two systems. It is nearly impossible to waste training dollars on these positions since they are so crucial, and training dollars need to be allocated for these positions.

Another role of software user is that of a heads-down user, typified by heavy use of a small part of the application software. While these individuals spend a rather large percentage of their days using the software, they spend it doing basically routine tasks. Perhaps they are entering purchase orders or creating journal entries to adjust general ledger balances. The organization is not counting on these people to define how the system is used over time. They have little responsibility, if any, beyond that of their basic, periodic processes. They require a different type of training, which is not available directly from PeopleSoft but which is essential for project success. To provide this intensive, targeted training, organizations must develop and hold training sessions that target specific roles of users. As these positions turn over, ready availabilty of this training will ensure that the expertise survives. The implementation team must plan for these training sessions and see to it that they are carried out at the appropriate time.

3.5.2 *Occasional or particular users*

The occasional user presents a different set of challenges to the implementation. These users are likely to only utilize one or two specific functions of the software. They do not use it every day and, in fact, may go weeks at a time without ever logging in. The implementation team should consider their needs and provide specific training to each individual. It is not worth the overhead of developing training programs for these users unless individual topics are common to many of them. By and large, the power users need to be assigned to train these users in their targeted functional areas. They should develop "cheat-sheet" guides and provide a copy of the user manual sections pertaining to each specific function. PeopleSoft's documentation is customizable and is a good starting point for the documentation. Organizations will need to develop training curricula to target commonly needed skills. One such skill is the ability to create simple nVision reports and to run existing reports and queries. A training session that demonstrates how to use nVision and then concentrates on how and where to look for guidance will be helpful. Since these users don't use the software every day, the focus must be on how to help them be self-sufficient, if not experts. Failure to do this will put a heavy strain on the power users in an organization, as they will be called upon to answer common questions over and over. With careful planning and effective training and reference materials, the occasional user can be mostly self-sufficient.

3.5.3 *Executives*

Paying too much attention to executives could lead them to micromanage the project, and paying them too little attention could result in terminated staff or a canceled project. The best way to manage executives is to keep them briefed on the project's status. Face-to-face briefings focusing on milestones and deliverables are most effective. Too much detail will lead to confusion and too many questions. They really just need to know what resources are assigned to the project, for how long, how effectively they are working, and what obstacles are in the way. Executive briefings should be planned by either the project manager or the executive sponsor. This will help keep them satisfied that their investment and resource allocations are making tangible progress. And, in the event that the project is mired in some political or organizational dilemma, they have a chance to act in time to save it. Many project teams overlook this key user area, but any successful team should proudly communicate the project status reports to top management. It provides an avenue of recognition for the project members as well.

3.5.4 Peripheral users

Other users, who only interact with the fringe of the software, will probably need no training at all—for example, users who read the department accounting reports will not need PeopleSoft training to understand them. They may need a memo explaining a format change or an orientation meeting to discuss potential new business rules affecting their areas, but no further training will be needed. Paradoxically, these uninvolved users can be the biggest problem in the organization. Failure to make them feel involved at some level can turn them into naysayers, who expend significant energy sabotaging the project's reputation. The implementation team should invite these people to participate in sessions explaining decisions, project status, and changes that might affect them. It is beneficial to ask for their input, even if it is ultimately not used. These people have been known to possess a good idea or two in the past, and they may raise an issue overlooked by the implementation team. One or two sessions throughout the duration of the implementation will suffice. It may seem to be a nuisance, but the implementation team should view it as a public relation effort and an opportunity to develop additional presentation and group facilitation skills.

3.5.5 End-user technical staff

The final group we will discuss is the end user technical specialists. These are the programmers located in the end user departments. If they are not involved in the implementation, they will need to receive technical training and functional training appropriate for their responsibility level and at the appropriate time. Typically, it is appropriate to send these people to PeopleTools training, SQR programming, and People-Soft Reporting training sessions. They should never attend a training session that they are not prepared to apply immediately. If they attend PeopleTools training, they should return and prototype some records and panels immediately. Many organizations will not allow these people to make changes to production, but they will be encouraged to prototype in a test database before requesting changes by central information systems developers.

Simple knowledge of the tools will not help these people unless they know the underlying application. For this reason, the technical experts on the implementation team need to be available to transfer their knowledge of the design of the applications. PeopleSoft sends a data model with its documentation. Using this model as a foundation should help educate these people about the structure of the database, so they will know where to look for specific information when their departments request reports from them. These people must absolutely understand the SQL programming language, table joins, and performance implications of particular SQL statements. They will be able to bring the database server performance to a screeching halt with a single, runaway statement. For this reason, they need to work closely with the central database staff to attain the appropriate level of access and CPU allocation.

The same rules that apply to the legacy programmer, discussed previously, may apply to some of these individuals. Some of them may not have the desire or ability to learn the new tools and techniques. If that is the case, the reporting function has to be put on the shoulders of someone else. However, assuming that these people are willing and able to learn, they can be a valuable resource for central information systems. They can be the level-one support for their departments. That lightens the support burden for the central help desk and also provides better service to the end users. The project team has to make provisions for these people and how best to leverage their skills and expertise to provide the maximum benefit for their departments.

We have seen the complexity of the PeopleSoft client/server software package and discussed the challenges it poses for the implementation team. In addition, we discussed the various roles in an organization and their degree of interaction with the software. It is clear that implementing a complex client/server software package presents significant training obstacles for organizations. Aside from the skills and make-up of the implementation team, it is the single largest factor affecting the success an organization will have assimilating the new software into its corporate culture. Organizations that skimp in this area are destined to install and utilize PeopleSoft suboptimally. Instead, they should plan to spend as much money on training as they spend on the actual software. Failure to do so will adversely affect the implementation of any complex software package, and PeopleSoft typifies this in grand fashion.

chapter 4

Implementation strategy

Presumably, if an organization has decided to purchase PeopleSoft Financials, it has done a comparison of the software against its competitors and negotiated and signed the contract with PeopleSoft. Now what? The process of selecting a software vendor may seem difficult, but it is only the beginning. Signing a contract provides no relief to the financial staff struggling to keep up with changing business requirements. What does the organization do next? How does the implementation project get off the ground? The next order of business is to erect the project's framework. It is to form the implementation team, develop the project plan, assess and manage the risks involved, and provide a means to communicate and update the project plan. When these building blocks are put in place, the project can then move forward.

Before we get into the specifics of formulating the project strategy, let's examine the extremes of software projects. On the one hand are the "hacks." They are known for cutting corners, hard-coding programs, and doing anything to meet deadlines. For them it is harder to provide long-term support, because the team is lax about standards and documentation. Software engineers detest projects that are so unstructured and undisciplined and for good reason. However, at the other extreme are these software engineers themselves. Their projects are a celebration of technology for its sake alone. The search for technical nirvana supersedes all other priorities. No excuse, neither time nor money, justifies violation of sacred software engineering principles. Data denormalization is scoffed at, and nothing is done until everything is done and done "right." The problem with this approach is that the project will probably never reach completion. It is perpetually in process, as the engineers struggle to perfectly match the moving target of business requirements. The key in formulating the strategy for the PeopleSoft implementation is to avoid these two extremes while drawing from the strengths of each. The implementation should be timely and efficient and, at the same time, appropriate standards and processes should be employed so as to ensure the long-term health of the software. This middle ground may be difficult to find, but it is critical for a successful project. The best way to guarantee it is to form an implementation team committed to this balance.

4.1 Form the implementation team

The individual asked to formally establish the implementation team has an extremely important job. The project's success will be a direct result of the team's ability to create, communicate, and execute an implementation strategy. The project team is made up of technical staff, end users, end user managers and executive sponsors. The project leader is the connector responsible for bridging the gaps between these groups to make a cohesive, working team. The team will work closely together for an extended period of time, so the members must actually like one another—at least professionally but preferably personally, too. Collectively, they should cover the full range of skills needed to implement the project. Of critical importance, too, is the choice of the team leader, since much of the responsibility will fall on that person's shoulders. Each of these issues must be carefully and methodically considered, with the final choices made to maximize the chance of success. If a productive working team is formed, and if it has the trust and support of executive

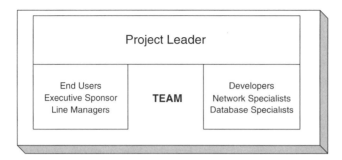

Figure 4.1 The implementation team

management, the organization can sit back with relative confidence that the implementation will succeed. (See Figure 4.1.)

4.1.1 Choose the right skills and the right people

It is intuitively obvious that the team must have the ability to accomplish the tasks involved in the implementation. Without the appropriate skills, it will never get off the ground. No organization with any common sense would form a team of incompetent people and expect it to implement PeopleSoft Financials. However, simply selecting the most competent technical people without matching end user expertise, for example, will create a situation where the team is too focused on technical issues. So, exactly how does one go about building the team? The key is to remember to look to the organizational goals—for example, if a professional basketball team has a strategic plan calling for a high-powered, fast-paced, high-scoring offense, that is critical information to consider when drafting and trading for the team members. It would be counterproductive to draft a large, slow-footed center when the team will need to run. That analogy holds true in determining the members of the implementation team. Be sure to align the makeup and specific skills and work styles with the organization's goals. If the organization wants to install the software with few customizations and do so quickly, then the team members should be good at finding innovative solutions and working in a fast-paced manner. If, on the other hand, the organization plans to heavily modify the software, the project team should be one that is more methodical and thorough in order to coordinate the intracacies involved.

Project leader   The most critical position on the team is that of the project leader. In cartoon language, this person must be 50 percent developer, 50 percent end user, 50 percent marketing specialist, and 50 percent hero, but mostly all psychologist. Project management has historically focused on the technical engineering principles associated with defining and monitoring the completion of the project tasks. More recently, however, project management experts have stressed the importance of the behavioral issues associated with projects. The project manager is more appropriately called the project leader, if the role's requirements are met correctly. Leadership is the key attribute required for this person. The project team will bring together executive sponsors, end users, end user management, and technical staff. The project leader must nurture these relationships. He or she must compile and communicate the formal project plan and is responsible for the traditional management tasks associated with its completion. This person also will negotiate with and report to executive management and market the project throughout the organization. Furthering our analogy, a professional basketball coach manages players earning much more than the coach does. He or she must utilize the strengths of these players, being careful to avoid causing resentment among them. The coach must keep the adminstration happy and must, at times, play public relations director with the press. And oh, by the way, the coach should have some technical knowledge of the game of basketball as well.

Key skills for a project leader include the following.

1   Confidence, competence and courage (3 Cs)

2   Team building, motivation, communication, and managerial skills

3   Supportive of staff—works side-by-side with them

4   Broad business sense and skills

Technical professionals chosen as project leaders are often predisposed to focus on and stress the importance of technology and formal engineering principles. A savvy project leader understands that this is but one aspect of the job at hand. An excellent way to help potential project leaders understand their roles is to look at the leadership of projects based on life and death. Ground control of the Apollo 13 mission is an awesome exaggeration of the issues facing today's project leaders. In basic terms, the project leader must know when to celebrate with the team, when to grieve with it, when to defend it, and when to attack it. He or she must know when to support executive management and when to stand up to it. The skills required are a blending of technical management capability and intuitive relationship building. Qualities to look for include having experience and success working in team situations including team sports; holding the respect of the team members and of executive management; being capable of intuitive thinking; possessing a track record of success; being competent with the technologies and business processes; and displaying confidence and humility. This is going to be a difficult combination of skills to find, but as many as possible need to be present in the team's leader.

Team members   Once the project leader is chosen, it is time to put together the individual team members. If possible, consult the project leader to be sure that he or she feels the team has the necessary skills. The level of involvement provided to the project leader should be based on his or her experience and capabilities. At the very least, though, the project leader should get a chance to review the team and raise any red flags before names are formally announced. Those responsible for picking the team members must focus on technical ability and knowledge, along with their ability to get along with each other. This team will work together for an extended period of time. It will face obstacles that will test the members' relationships and their ability to stay focused and work through conflicts. Avoid putting people with known personality conflicts together, unless it is certain that they will overcome their problems. Aside from these issues, it is critical to fully staff each of the remaining roles of the project team.

Executive sponsor   One key role is that of the executive sponsor. More than likely, that individual has been involved with and may even be the driving force behind the PeopleSoft Financials purchase, so the choice is made up front, which can be a problem. The executive sponsor is most often someone of higher rank in the organization and may even exceed the project leader's pay grade by three or more levels; however, the day-to-day management and direction of the project falls on the shoulders of the project leader, not the executive sponsor. This must be made clear from the outset. Typically, this is a win-win situation, because the executive sponsor is likely to be too busy to do it anyway. There is the potential for power plays, however, and avoiding them is important. The function of the executive sponsor is, in a sense, to be the "big stick." This person has a vested interest and the clout to make the tough organizational decisions. This person will deflect the criticism from the project team and claim responsibility for the major decisions that affect the organization. At the same time, this person must avoid claiming responsibility for successes on behalf of the team. It is also important for the executive sponsor to be available to commit the time required to attend the meetings and to communicate throughout the organization when necessary. He or she will work closely with the project leader to set priorities and develop strategy, so a good working relationship between the two is also vital.

Line manager   Another role essential to the formation of an effective team is the line manager. Line managers are the functional managers who will be responsible for the day-to-day operation of the software and the department, once they are implemented. As such, their input to the development process is invaluable. They probably have the best understanding of the department's current business processes and procedures. The project team needs buy-in from the department and that must start from the top with the line manager. This person will be challenged to meet the obligations of the implementation and to serve in a traditional role as the department's manager. If possible, organizations should strive to free the line manager's time to dedicate as much as possible to the software implementation project.

End users   Joining the functional line manager on the team will be actual end users. We have used the term "power users," and this term applies to these people as well. Not all staff, not even most staff, will serve on the team. Those who are most knowledgeable and who will hold most responsibility on a daily basis ought to be included, however. Again, organizations should relieve the end users of as many of their normal duties as possible. If they are involved and working on the project along with the line manager, the project team can hold a decidedly end user point of view. At different times in the implementation, the team will probably bring in additional end users to answer particular questions or examine individual processes. These extra, part time members are not considered part of the formal team; otherwise, the team risks being too large to be efficient.

Technical staff On the technical side of the team are the programmers, network support specialists, and database administrators. Some people may fill more than one of these roles. If so, the database administrator and the network specialist can be floating positions; these people do not attend all team meetings and functions, but are formally assigned to the project. Their time and effort requirements will ebb and flow as the stages of the implementation unfold. By and large, the programmers should go to all of the meetings in order to gain the understanding of the processes discussed and the reasons and ramifications of the customization requests. Again, it is critical for the programming members of the team to be aligned with the goals established for the project. If a legacy programmer is included on the team, he or she must be offset by one or more programmers familiar with client/server, Microsoft Windows development, graphical user interfaces, and relational database systems. The PeopleSoft implementation is an excellent opportunity to jump-start a legacy programmer into the new paradigm, due to the intense training and heads-down attention common in major system installations.

With all the different roles on the team, organizations may find themselves susceptible to being too concerned with the individual team members at the expense of the team itself. While each of these roles is critical and has to be cast with the best and brightest, it cannot be at the expense of the implementation strategy or the organization's goals for the project. Before finalizing the members of the team, they should be judged against a list of attributes needed for the team—for example, if the organization wants to install the software with major customizations, which are complex and critical, a list of attributes for the team might be: methodical, thorough, adheres to standards, values testing and quality assurance. Upon selecting a team member, a quick run-through of these criteria will guard against assigning a "loose cannon" programmer to the team. Assuming all of the members can work within the context of the project goals and their personalities do not clash, the team should be ready, willing, and able to begin its arduous task.

The first order of business for the team should be some level of introspection. It should meet, formally, in short order and lay the groundwork for the project. Of utmost importance is the formal, mutually accepted assignment of roles and responsibilities. Nothing saps the productivity from a team faster than confusion as to responsibility. As much as possible, the project leader, executive sponsor, and organization in general should frame these decisions for the team, but at no time should they be dictated to the team. This team has to be led and to be led it must be willing to follow. To that end, the team members must be part of the decision-making process from the beginning. Now, with the team in place and the individual roles and responsibilities clear, the team is prepared to take its first major step in the implementation: developing the project plan.

4.2 Develop the project plan

The project plan is a risky endeavor in and of itself. The plan is just a list of milestones, tasks, relationships, and responsibilities on a few sheets of paper. That paper carries with it the power to transform the careers of the team members. Indeed, the team's performance may be measured against the standards put forth in the plan. It is critical that this task be approached seriously, methodically, and carefully. It is human nature for people to oversimplify projects that are enormous. According to a 1994 survey conducted by the Standish Group, only 16 percent of software projects succeed in completing on time within budget. In fact, 31 percent of projects are complete failures, being either canceled along the way or completed but not functional enough to be put into use. Implementing PeopleSoft Financials is a monumental task. It is exceedingly difficult. The sheer magnitude of the changes is overwhelming, and the team must be certain that it is capable of meeting the established target dates.

On the other side of the coin is the watchful eye of the organization's senior management. Inevitably, they are the ones who have bitten the bullet and written the check committing to the expense and hardship of the implementation. Presumably, management knows that the implementation is worth it to the organization and will support the team in every way possible, but a team that is too cautious may shake the confidence of those at the executive level. Too often, these high-level managers know enough about personal computers to think they understand corporate software implementations. They will not be receptive to an open-ended project plan. They must see committed target dates that are reasonable in their own minds. Truthfully, almost any target date will seem excessively far out to those not accustomed to complex management information systems. The project plan needs to be structured to identify deliverables at frequent intervals so as to assure management that it will have an opportunity to monitor its progress and to intervene if the implementation stalls. If the team gives the project plan proper attention, it can be the vehicle by which the team informs the rest of the organization of the structure and status of the implementation.

The plan itself will vary dramatically from organization to organization. It is not practical to present a detailed project plan here. It is important, however, to focus on the key elements of the plan.

4.2.1 Key plan elements

Only estimate what you know   Optimistic developers especially are prone to committing to a target date without proper up-front analysis. For an isolated task this is not significant, but when it is multiplied by the number of tasks in a PeopleSoft implementation, the potential margin of error is described in terms of months. The experienced project leader estimates only when he or she has enough information to be confident with the estimate. The project team needs to gain and keep the confidence of the organization and, particularly, executive management. Consistently meeting projected dates is one sure way to do that. Conversely, consistently missing dates is certain to ruin the team's reputation and jeopardize the project's success. The project team must not schedule later stages of the project that rely on the outcomes of earlier stages. In spite of pressure to do so, it must firmly refuse to estimate without proper analysis.

Commit to the estimates   Once the team publishes an estimate, the members must commit to it. Finishing it ahead of schedule buys slack time for the project team. Since missing the date is not an option, when it appears that a task will not be finished by its target date, the assigned team members will have to work overtime. For this reason, it is wise to schedule target dates on Friday, so staff has Saturday and Sunday as a two-day buffer. Of course, it is more desirable to meet the original date, so the staff has a chance for rejuvenation on the weekends.

Keep the tasks small enough to manage   The success with which a project team meets target dates is directly related to the size of the tasks themselves. Many students of project management strongly urge project leaders to limit any single task's effort to two weeks. The margin of error is too large with tasks exceeding two weeks. They should be broken into smaller tasks of two weeks or under. Each of these tasks can be framed as deliverables, which gives the project leader a number of accomplishments for each progress report.

Guard against "magician syndrome"   In the spectacular tradition of the master magician who pulls a rabbit out of a hat, executive management is famous for pulling dates out of a hat. The project leader must protect the team from this approach. The truth is, a date pulled out of thin air is possibly too far out as opposed to not far enough out. Using this uncertainty, the project leader can preempt this tendency as long as the alternative is reasonable and puts the ultimate decision with these people. Given the nature of organizational politics, the executive sponsor and the project leader must form a united front. The best way to insure that logically derived dates are not overthrown on a whim is to include the different possible strategies and their corresponding implications, costs, benefits, and target dates together with the team's recommended approach. When the project plan is put into business terminology and justified using cost/benefit analysis, it is highly probable that executive management will support the project plan as presented by the team.

On the other hand, an organization may find that it has no choice but to set a date based on some circumstances out of its control. While this is less than ideal, when it happens, the date itself will have to structure the project's implementation strategy. In this case, the project team must clearly articulate the impact that the date will have on the implementation. When a project faces immense time pressures, it will be forced to replace planned, effective strategies with new ones based solely on implementation speed. When the software is cut over to production, the team has to be able to replace those components and procedures with more stable ones. It is essential for the project team to negotiate this up front, or it will be whisked away to another project, leaving a production support headache for the organization.

Commit to a phased approach   The term "phased" can mean different things to different people in varying circumstances. One thing it does, irrespective of its specific approach, is break up the project into manageable parts. Phasing the project also offers the organization concrete, major deliverables sooner, so the organization benefits with improvements earlier on. This often translates into cost-justification, which executive management readily understands. The converse of a phased approach occurs when the team implements the entire project, including conversion and customizations, into production at one time. While it is not the purpose of this book to explain the theories and methods of project management, there is a wealth of information available supporting the assertion that a phased approach has a greater likelihood of success. Project studies demonstrate that the greater the number of person-months of effort a project requires, the longer it will take to implement, regardless of the number of people involved—for example, a ten-person-month project may take three people four months to complete. Two ten-person-month projects would, therefore, take three people eight months to complete. However, a single twenty-person-month project might take the same three people ten months to finish. The specific theories and formulas are readily available, but, focusing on the concepts, it is clear that phasing the project can shorten the overall implementation.

Phase I:

- Analyze current business processes
- Prototype the new system & indentify customization requirements

Phase II:

- Data conversion
- Code customizations—all Priority I, many Priority II
- Build interfaces
- Integration testing
- Production cutover

Phase III:

- Postimplementation production support
- Documentation and clean up
- Remaining Priority II customizations

Figure 4.2 Sample high-level phased project plan

A phased project plan does have one major drawback. Specifically, the phases at the end of the project plan can fall prey to other priorities. The project leader must communicate to the organization the reasons behind the final phases and the long-term consequences of neglecting them. It is a common occurrence for Phase III of software projects to remain incomplete for years. The reality is that these final phases end up being completed as production support, putting an additional strain on staff at a time when workloads may already be high. Again, communicating this to executive management is critical. The team needs to negotiate this up front to avoid conflict later. (See Figure 4.2.)

Prioritize requirements   It is an unfortunate reality that estimating software implementation tasks is a tricky and not very well done process. The problems are many and some are even understandable. If we accept it as a reality, we must then formulate a strategy to minimize the impact of this margin of error. One such strategy is prioritization. Most adaptations are variations of a similar theme. All implementation tasks, particularly software customizations but also others, once identified, are assigned one of three priorities. Priority I tasks are those that must be completed before the software can be put into production. Priority II tasks are those that are necessary or highly desirable but can be delayed until the phase following production cutover. Priority III tasks are nice-to-have "requirements" which probably will never be completed. Using this strategy, the project team focuses on the Priority I tasks—completing all of them and then squeezing in as many Priority II tasks as possible before the production cutover date. This has the effect of creating "working slack time" and relieving some of the pressure from the implementation during the crunch periods.

Avoid scope creep—establish a change budget   There are two major tendencies that threaten the success of any major software implementation, including PeopleSoft Financials. One is the search for technical nirvana on the part of the technical staff. The other one is scope creep. Scope creep is defined as the intentional or informal addition of requirements into the project after the specifications were agreed upon by the customers and the project team. Scope creep, when unmanaged, can devastate a software implementation. Programmers have always been susceptible to it because they enjoy adding features and functionality. It is their job—their raison d'être. Many project management experts assert that scope creep is the single biggest killer of software implementation projects. It is up to the project leader to make certain that requirements changes are official and managed.

Table 4.2 Reasons for late/over budget projects

Percent	Reasons why projects are "challenged" (late/over budget)
12.8%	Lack of user input
12.3%	Incomplete requirements and specifications
11.8%	Changing requirements and specifications
7.5%	Lack of executive support
7.0%	Technology incompetence
6.4%	Lack of resources
5.9%	Unrealistic expectations
5.3%	Unclear objectives
4.3%	Unrealistic time frames
3.7%	New technology

Table 4.1 Reasons for Project Failure

Percent	Reason Why Projects Fail
13.1%	Incomplete requirements
12.4%	Lack of user involvement
10.6%	Lack of resources
9.9%	Unrealistic expectations
9.3%	Lack of executive support
8.7%	Changing requirements and specifications
8.1%	Lack of planning
7.5%	Didn't need the software any longer
6.2%	Lack of IT management
4.3%	Technology illiteracy

One way to manage scope creep is to establish a change budget for the project. In other words, suppose a project will take six months to complete and, based upon various risk factors and organizational flexibility, the project can safely be completed in anywhere between six and eight months. The project team might establish a change budget of two months. Then, any requirements added, becoming scope creep, are formally approved and charged against the change budget. Once the change budget is expended, no further requirements can be added. This keeps the end users from adding features without first justifying them to the team and to their departments, and it clarifies their impact on the project timeline.

These strategies are but a few that project leaders can use to guard against a failed project. They happen to be ones that are important for a PeopleSoft Financials implementation, but there are dozens more. Individual project teams must evaluate their current organizational pressures to employ others as needed. To help understand the mechanics of projects and why they fail, it is again helpful to quote the results of the 1994 Standish Group's survey of project success. The survey revealed several reasons for project failures. (See Table 4.1 and Table 4.2.)

The team implementing PeopleSoft Financials will face many pressures. Project management is an art—a science and a psychology—and the study of it is a career-long process. However, if the project plan is properly structured and defensible, it won't be used as a weapon against the team. Small tasks, estimated only when all essential information is available, combined with a phased approach will leave room for the project team to be responsive and productive and allow it to provide deliverables at regular intervals for excellent visibility.

4.3 Assess and manage the risk

In an information systems project in general, and especially in a People-Soft implementation, the project team is in a precarious situation. The team has the responsibility for successfully installing and deploying leading-edge software throughout the organization. We've discussed some of the potential obstacles, but we have not talked about the consequences of missing perfection. And, further, we've not identified who is responsible to pay those consequences. All too often, it falls to the implementation team. It is reasonable to believe that if a software project fails, it must be due to technical problems or incompetent programming staff. After a little research, however, it becomes clear that failures are most often not due to technical problems, but to poor project management as a whole. The team faces the difficult challenge of navigating a landmine of potential roadblocks to success. Poor project management will almost certainly guarantee a sloppy or failed project, but even one that is well planned and properly managed can leave a team as political scapegoats. When this happens, it is because the project team has not effectively assessed and managed the risks involved.

Risk assessment is an intricate and tedious science. One could spend a career on the topic. In a practical sense, however, project teams need a mechanism for identifying the likely risk variables and for safeguarding themselves against the consequences of circumstances and decisions out of their control. They need a means to do these things quickly and efficiently, so they can move on to the actual implementation. Specifically, the team needs to identify all of the likely risk variables and what their corresponding impact ranges are. Once this information is centralized, the team can target specific actions to mitigate each risk factor. Then, these risks can be communicated to executive management, so they can agree to share the risk with the project team.

In identifying the risk variables, the team should only focus on those risk factors that are fairly likely to occur. If the probability of an earthquake taking out the corporate network is only .00125 percent, it is not cost effective to formulate an avoidance strategy for that factor. Conversely, if it is reasonably probable that end users will not be relieved from their current workloads to concentrate on the implementation project, then this risk factor must be articulated and included in the project plan. Once it is identified, the next step is to state the assumption of the project team with respect to the specific factor. In our end user availability example, the assumption might be that all end users assigned to the project team will be free to devote 30 hours each week to the implementation. Then, negative and positive range outcomes can be identified—for example, the negative impact definition is that the staff is not relieved of its normal duties and is not able to define requirements and assure quality test results, adding two months to the implementation. The positive impact is that the staff is available full time, shortening the project by two weeks. Finally, for each risk factor identified, the team should formulate an avoidance strategy. Avoidance strategies will usually involve the commitment and cooperation of other departments and/ or executive management. When these strategies are formally identified in this way, executive management, by not refuting the assertions, is conceptually agreeing to share in the risks. In this way, everyone knows, before the project is underway, what factors will endanger the project's success. The project team will not face an inquisition when a specific factor affects the implementation, and, in fact, it will be able to pull out the project plan and say, "I told you so!" When they are issued tactfully, "I told you so's" can build organizational trust in the team, helping it in future projects.

An example of a project risk assessment worksheet is shown in Table 4.3. Notice how it brings together the various aspects of each risk factor into a single, easily digested format, which can be shared and understood by everyone in an organization. It is extremely helpful if the negative and positive impact columns are represented graphically with, for example, bar chart-type values. Then the potential impact of all the risk factors is easy to see and understand. That summarized range can be used as a basis for establishing the projects change budget. Assessing the project risk in this format can clarify potential pitfalls and help to rally the troops to safeguard against them. It can be done in only a few hours, allowing the project team to quickly move on to its next task.

4.4 Communicate the plan

The world's greatest implementation strategy is worthless if it is not effectively and appropriately communicated throughout the organization. The absolute worst thing a project team can do in today's business climate is to go off into a cave and work in obscurity, planning to return on a white horse to save the day. A major client/server system such as PeopleSoft Financials carries a high price tag, and executive management will need assurance that its multimillion dollar investment is not being squandered. So exactly how does the team communicate the project plan?

The obvious answer is to share it with those affected. It is imperative that it be in a format that is readily understood by its individual audiences. For most purposes, a Gantt chart of the project phases and tasks is a good starting point. However, it should not assign resources or estimates to tasks that are not yet fully defined and analyzed—for example, the first iteration of the project plan might have project start up, current process diagramming, and prototyping estimated and assigned to staff. Those tasks would have an associated Gantt chart, with horizontal bars representing a starting and ending point. Tasks such as data conversion, interface building, and customizations cannot be estimated until their analysis is complete, so they should only have a relative position on the plan and dependencies to other tasks. This format is easy to grasp and busy executives will appreciate its brevity.

To support the detailed, estimated section of the Gantt chart, the distributed plan should include specification forms for each task. This may seem excessive, but, in reality, unless politics have set it up as the "fall guy," the team cannot provide too much information. The more details are shared throughout the organization, the more protected the team is and the more likely it is that problems will be caught early in the project, saving time and effort in the long run. The project leader should be brutally honest when discussing the project plans because, regardless of whether or not everyone agrees, honesty and constancy do engender trust and professional respect.

So far, the Gantt chart and specifications have been included in the communicated project packet. The next piece of information to add to the set is the risk assessment profile, as discussed in Section 4.3. Assuming that it is not overdone, it ought to be on one or two pages, and it should be easy to understand. At this point, it may seem that enough is enough. However, one vital aspect of the project is missing, and it is crucial to instill it in the organization: the vision. Joel Barker, futurist and author of "Future Edge," says, "Vision without action is only dreaming, and action without vision merely passes the time. But vision with action can change the world." Powerful assertions, yet simple at heart. People need to know what they are doing and why they are doing it, and they need to feel included in the process. It is important when implementing People-Soft Financials to garner supporters from all levels of the organization. The project vision can set the tone and provide the context in which the project plan fits. The project vision is best included as part of a cover memo attached to the project plan. It should be brief, focusing on the end state of the project.

So, hours of effort and collaboration will yield five or ten pages of summarized project information and several pages of detailed require-ments. In a single, concise medium, the entire course of the project is laid out for all to see. It is readily apparent who is assigned what resonsibil-ity, what specific requirements are defined, and what the vision of the project is. The specifics of the plan's distribution will depend on the orga-nization. Some may want a formal presentation. Others will use inter-campus mail and send it to all but the most involved members. Some

Table 4.3 Sample risk assessment worksheet

Risk Factor	Project Expectations	Worst Case	Best Case	Negative Impact	Positive Impact	Avoidance Strategy
Technical staff availability	Technical staff is 100% dedicated to the project.	Technical staff is routinely pulled off for other projects.	Technical staff is 100% dedicated to the project.	+8 Weeks	0	Hire contract programmers to support legacy systems.
New technology	The new technology will have only a few snags.	The new technology is unstable and requires much debugging.	New technology has no snags and is absorbed rapidly.	+3 Weeks	-2 Weeks	Schedule ample training and order technical documentation.
Availability of executive sponsor	Sponsor will be available and responsive throughout.	Not available. Decisions require multiple phone calls and meetings.	Project is sponsor's major priority.	+4 Weeks	-1 Week	Notify organization that sponsor will be less available to others throughout the project.

may even install it on an "intranet" Web server for access by all in the organization. Whatever the means, the team should be reasonably secure that executive management has received and digested the materials thoroughly enough to sanction the project and its direction. As the implementation unfolds and the project plan develops more fully, perhaps as the team completes each phase, the project leader must update this report and redistribute it. This may seem like tedious work, but it is time well spent. When executive management asks a question, the project team will have the information to answer swiftly and consistently, again creating trust and respect.

4.4.1 Status reports

Another key component of a well-run, PeopleSoft project is regular status reports. Nobody likes to create status reports, because they are time-consuming and often not used; however, they can be a powerful tool, protecting the implementation team politically while providing valuable information to executive management and the organization as a whole. It is a good idea to establish the expectations at the outset and ensure that the implementation team consistently produces the status reports.

Technically, there are two different types of status reports with which we are concerned. One is the operational status report and the other is the project status report. The operational status reports are created by the technical staff in the course of completing implementation tasks. The nontechnical members can also produce status reports, assuming they are responsible for completing tasks of the project plan. The report should be very brief, and it should focus on completed tasks, progress on tasks in process, and identification of tasks soon to begin. Also, any problems, concerns, or obstacles encountered should be noted, so they can be addressed by the project leader and the rest of the team. A sample operational status report might look like that shown in Figure 4.3.

The operational reports can often be generated manually by the project management system used by the implementation team. If that is at all possible, it is highly desirable. If they must be created manually, then the project leader must stress the value of the reports and strive to make them steamlined and easy to do. By sharing these reports, the entire team can keep tabs on the progress of others, creating an excellent

---

Status Report for Bill Belitz
August 8–August 15

Tasks Completed

1 Coded/tested APY3409.SQR—new 1099 vendors report

2 Applied PeopleSoft Patch GN-RAMAK-89 for invalid operator ID error

3 Completed modification of the Crystal Checks layout, including MICR and signature lines

Progress

1 Started coding voucher reference number queries

Notables

1 Overflow handling for checks does not appear to work as we'd hoped. We'll need to ask end users if vanilla process is acceptable or add a customization request.

Figure 4.3 Sample operational status report

information-sharing process without requiring time-consuming team meetings during times of extremely heavy workloads.

The other type of status report is a little more formal and much more visible. It is the project status report, which communicates the project's progress to the executive management and the organization. It must be formal, concise, and easy to digest. An updated Gantt chart and a one- or two-page memo outlining the major decisions and their impacts on the project as well as major accomplishments is all that is required. Table 4.4 shows the differences between operational status reports and project status reports.

The specific timings, methods, and format of the status reporting process is up to each organization and each project leader's style. As much as possible, it should be automated. The critical components of the status reporting process are that it occurs at regular intervals and that it can be digested easily by the intended audience. Status reports help to flood the organization with information and protect the implementation team from being blamed for surprise decisions. With a clearly documented

Table 4.4 Operational status reports versus project status reports

Operational Status Report	Project Status Report
Target audience is project leader	Refocuses the project team
Functions as "to-do" list for team members	Target audience is executive management
Should identify obstacles	Highlights major decisions
Lists completed tasks	Identifies "problem" risk factors
Lists progress on tasks not complete	
Lists tasks scheduled to start	

paper trail of all major decisions and problems, the team is more insulated from organizational politics.

4.5 Problems and opportunities

We've discussed issues of project management that have application for almost any project, but that are especially effective for PeopleSoft implementations. Project leaders, however, will want to know what the special problems and opportunities facing PeopleSoft implementation project teams are. So let's examine some of these common obstacles

4.5.1 Implementation obstacles

Demanding project leadership requirements The complex nature of PeopleSoft Financials automatically makes it challenging for the project leader. Leaving out the impact it will have on the organization as a whole, the technical scope will demand a great deal of planning and coordination on the part of the project leader. The implementation, especially if it is replacing a legacy system, will upset the lives and jobs of many people throughout the organization. The project leader must be experienced at planning and coordinating all of the technologies and relationships. It is a major blunder to assign an inexperienced project manager to run a PeopleSoft implementation without experienced guidance to assist him.

Cool technology creates the wrong focus   There is no doubt that PeopleSoft Financials is "cool" technology. Developers and end users alike are enamored with the technology. It is easy for developers to get lost in the technology and forget that it is a vendor package. Every modification that the developers make to the system will require rework when the software is upgraded. If they are not controlled, they can easily go overboard, jumping at every whim of the end users. This wrong technical focus is a major factor in less than ideal implementations. The project leader and executive sponsor must monitor this issue.

Unwillingness to change business rules   PeopleSoft software presents a rare opportunity for organizations to reengineer their businesses to better meet the needs of internal and external customers. However, it is not something that is easy to do in many organizations. Especially in parts of the organization that are not familiar with software implementation and that do not see the "Peoplesoft Paradigm," project teams may find significant resistance to change. This can be exceedingly difficult to overcome and may even require that the project leader enlist the support of executive management. It is politically tricky, but essential, to get buy-in supporting these business shakeups.

Stress   Okay, so all software projects are stressful. Most experienced software developers can tell you that. But the nature of PeopleSoft implementations can be excessively grueling. The massive organizational change and the technical complexity puts enormous pressure on the project team. In many ways it can be a career-changing project for the entire implementation team. The scope and complexity of the new processes and technologies will challenge the technical staff's capacity to learn while keeping the project on track. It is not unheard of, either, for project teams to put in 70 or 80 hours each week during peak periods, so judgment can become impaired and relationships can become strained. Again, the project leader is responsible for monitoring the stress levels and taking appropriate action when required.

New technology in old organizations   In organizations that are new to client/server, the sudden transition PeopleSoft will bring with it will be a culture shock. This is not entirely bad, but it does need to be recognized and addressed. It may require additional training, a longer implementation, or hiring technical consultants. Organizations that have significant LAN, client/server, and database expertise will not feel as much pain, but those who don't will face significant learning curves simply to support the software.

Deployment options   PeopleSoft financials is designed to put information into the hands of the appropriate people, when and where they need it. An organization could literally put PeopleSoft on the desktop of every employee. That is obviously neither cost-effective nor logistically possible, but somewhere between that extreme and the more typical group of elite power users resides the true optimum number of end users throughout the organization. Determining this number is a challenging task. There is no right or wrong answer, except that it should meet the organization's goals. The real acid test is to ask this question: Are the people who need financial information able to access it effectively and in the appropriate time frame? With this as a guide, the infusion of PeopleSoft workstations throughout the organization will probably continue over time until the organization reaches the most efficient deployment level. The project team must lay the groundwork for the continued, systematic distribution of the client workstations as warranted; otherwise, organizations may neglect the issue once the software is in production.

Unacceptable stress-test performance   Client/server systems in general, when they cut over to production, are often not very well stress tested. There are so many variables in the performance equation of PeopleSoft that no reliable performance predictions can be made without thorough testing. Waiting until too late in the project can seriously undermine the target date, because if the high-volume, high-stress testing reveals inadequate performance, the technical staff will have an undetermined amount of research and tuning to do before the system is production-ready. The worst-case scenerio would require even additional hardware. This is not likely, however, assuming the implementation team has the PeopleSoft account manager review the hardware and software platform and capacity plans early in the project.

Difficulty in diagnosing technical problems   Again, due to the technical complexities of the technology, when the software fails, finding out why can be tedious and troublesome. It often requires that programmers, database administrators, and network specialists work closely together to pinpoint exactly what the problem is. This is probably a benefit, because it starts these groups of support people working together in ways they perhaps never have. That in itself will benefit the organization. It is clear, however, that an adequate supply of expertise must be readily at hand.

Opportunity to learn from the experts   One of the most difficult aspects of a PeopleSoft implementation is learning the technical and functional interworkings of the software. It is exceedingly difficult for a project team to take an application as complex as this and digest it in a reasonable amount of time. Without the background of the software's paradigm, the project team is prone to making assumptions that could undermine the effort. It is much more expensive to reverse a bad decision than it is to pay to do the right thing from the outset. The popularity of PeopleSoft applications has given rise to a thriving "implementation partner" market. Organizations should enlist the help of an appropriate firm. It can jump-start the project, allow for efficient transfer of knowledge from the partner firm, and take some of the pressure off the project team. There really is no good reason to omit a third-party involvement, unless the organization has no real time-pressure for the project's completion date. In this case, the project team can take its time, relatively speaking, and learn about the software as it goes. Even in this situation, it is wise for the organization to review the project plan and strategy as it is gearing up. This experienced perspective can, for a relatively small sum, help to ensure that the project starts off in the direction that suits the particular circumstances. In any event, hiring consultants is a risky proposition and therefore requires a good deal of attention to detail if it is to meet with success.

chapter 5

Choosing an implementation partner

Probably the hardest thing for the implementation team is learning exactly how the entire suite of PeopleSoft Financials software works, how it integrates, what the processes are, and how they interrelate. There are literally thousands of configurations that could work for any organization. To understand all the parameters and their associated implications for the organization is an enormous undertaking. The organization *will* know how its business units operate—or at least they'll have the wherewithal to figure it out. So, there is a sort of communication gap between the business rules and the "PeopleSoft rules." Bridging this gap is a daunting task, yet it is one that must be completed in order for organizations to make full use of the software.

It is rather like providing a car to a skilled driver, placing him or her in unfamiliar territory, and telling this person to drive to a specific city. The driver has no idea where he or she is or how to find the destination. The driver does know, however, how to operate the vehicle. At best, he or she can hope to drive around, and eventually arrive at the destination.

However, give the driver a roadmap and he or she can very quickly plan a route to the destination and will waste little time reaching it. The People-Soft expertise is our analogy's "roadmap." Most organizations will have a limited understanding of the working of the PeopleSoft applications. Those with enough time can have their staffs make the effort to learn the functional intricacies, using a combination of product walk throughs, interaction with other PeopleSoft customers, and so forth. However, a much more efficient means of gaining the expertise is to enlist the help of those who have been there before. The market has developed a group of expert PeopleSoft consultants and implementation partners. This group is talented but small. Rapid growth has maintained a steady shortage. For that reason, organizations that can take advantage of these experts must use care to ensure that their money is well spent. Inflated prices and shortage of experts leaves the door wide open for less-qualified consultants to pose as experts. With proper planning, however, appropriate personnel can be found.

5.1 Consultant roles

In the software industry, and information technology in general, there are many independent consultants available to assist on almost any project. Consultants typically charge a relatively high rate, often an hourly one. This high wage and relatively low long-term stress entice professionals of all capabilities and experience levels to join the ranks of the independents. Depending on the background of a specific consultant or firm, the implementation team can use these specialists to fill a number of different project roles. Matching a consultant with an inappropriate or undefined role will at best waste money and possibly undermine the goals of the implementation team. Let's examine the roles that an independent might fill.

5.1.1 Project management

Of all the roles in the a PeopleSoft project, project management is the most critical. Many organizations, especially those that find themselves in the midst of their first client/server software implementation, are not equipped to handle the rigors of such a high-profile project—one that can have an enormous impact on the future of the organization. They might not have a risk-taker who is willing to put his or her career on the line to lead an inexperienced group. In this case, it is logical to hire an experienced PeopleSoft implementation firm to manage the project.

The project management consultant is more appropriately called a "PeopleSoft implementation partner." The PeopleSoft "subculture" fancies itself a fan of teamwork, and so the truly sanctioned PeopleSoft consulting firms are dubbed implementation partners. The early days of PeopleSoft Financials saw the emergence of a few, core partnering firms—namely, Ramos & Associates, BIT, The Applications Group, and others. These firms cut their corporate teeth helping organizations implement PeopleSoft, so they possess a wealth of experience and knowledge. They have a significant body of project management expertise from which to draw. Organizations that deem it necessary to contract for project management services should look closely at the history and experience of the consulting firm as well as the individual consultants themselves. Everybody and their brother has hung out a PeopleSoft consulting sign, and those with only a few implementations under their belts will do more harm than good.

The project management consulting firm should take a leadership role in the structure and execution of the project. They should not be expected to do the project themselves. In fact, the better firms would refuse to work on a project that is not adequately staffed by the organization. Application software needs care and feeding. A top priority for both the partnering firm and the project team should be the transfer of knowledge.

Goals for a project management partnering firm include the following.

- Set project expectations
- Establish project structure and schedule
- Execute the project plan
- Transfer knowledge to the organization

Organizations can find an implementation partner to provide the project management skills and to provide the required number of additional consultants on the more technical or functional side. The synergy from this package of consultants can give a project team a major jumpstart. Leveraging the experience of those who have the most experience is the easiest way to achieve a rapid implementation. However, there are some problems. First, it can be difficult to hire one of the experienced firms because they, like everyone else, cannot keep up with the demand. They may have a waiting list of a few weeks or a few months. Without ample notification, organizations may not find a firm that can supply the appropriate personnel within an acceptable time frame. Another problem is the shortage of experienced personnel. Because of this, the organization that hires an implementation partner runs the risk of getting a less-qualified group of consultants. Besides these two issues, these types of firms are likely to be the most expensive to hire. That is not to say they are not worth it, because they are. However, not all organizations can afford to hire them. Those that can, however, can achieve the highest project success levels.

5.1.2 Project review

Another potential role that a consultant might fill is to review the project for an organization and identify areas that need attention. This can be an excellent reality check. It assumes that the in-house staff possesses the necessary skills to complete the project. The review should encompass the structure of the team, the actual project tasks and timelines, the technology assumptions, training plans, and deployment strategy. It should identify areas of concern and major risks. A project review can be completed in a relatively short period of time. It is an expensive yet valuable service. The short duration of the review keeps the price tag within reach of most organizations.

5.1.3 Technical assistance

One of the first tasks facing a PeopleSoft customer is to assess the technical infrastructure of the organization and to evaluate the technical expertise of the staff. Upon completing this, many will find that they are ill-equipped to deal with the difficulties that client/server software will bring to the organization on a technical level. Depending on the scope of deployment and the logistics of the organization, ensuring that the technical environment is ready to support PeopleSoft can be a time-consuming effort. It may not be realistic to pile that much work on an already loaded technical staff. In addition, those people may need intense training to be able to manage such an environment, let alone plan and implement one. For this type of organization, technical consulting can provide significant benefits. The three major areas of technical assistance are networking, local area network management, and relational database management. Any or all of these can be appropriate.

The complexities of networking can range from moderate to monumental. A multinational firm with many locations that wishes to decentralize the use of the PeopleSoft applications poses significant networking issues. On the other hand, if it were to only deploy the applications to a single location, supporting it would be much less complex. The same is true of the LAN management and database management issues. The more that PeopleSoft is deployed, the more savvy the technical staff must be. Technical assistance can be purchased from a number of sources. The organization must take care that they are appropriately skilled, however. PeopleSoft can provide the technical requirements and present options. It is up to the organization to implement them. As long as the consultants are experienced in the technology and are contractually obliged to provide successful installation of the technology, there should be few problems in this area. It is wise to carefully define success before signing a contract. At the very least, all network links and database links should demonstrably operate. More than likely they will contractually only need to operate—that is, contractually, getting PeopleSoft to operate across them is likely to be beyond the scope of the technical experts. The PeopleSoft installation team will see to it that their applications function over the technical environment as long as that environment is appropriately set up.

5.1.4 Application design

Putting project management aside, application design is perhaps the most beneficial role that an organization can fill with a third-party contractor. PeopleSoft Professional Services has numerous talented and experienced application experts. They are highly proficient at spending a limited amount of time, usually a few weeks, and helping the project team determine how to use PeopleSoft applications within the context of their organization. Having this consultant around at key design decision points can save untold hours of customization, paying dividends for years. This is where the expertise of the consultant is most important. Only those who know the intricacies of such a complex system can successfully fill the role. Those consultants who have a reputation as being such an expert are highly sought after. It can be difficult to get a spot in their schedule. In addition, they charge perhaps the highest rates, often exceeding $200 per hour. However, it is well worth the price. Finding a good consultant to fill this role can only be done via the grapevine. By using PeopleSoft's Forum database, list serves, contacts at other sites, and by searching them out at the PeopleSoft User Conference, good consultants can be found. Once one is identified and hired, the organization should strive to use the same consultant over the life of the implementation. The consultant's closeness to the product and its direction, together with his or her experience with the organization, gives the consultant a perspective that every organization needs.

5.1.5 Programming resources

The easiest consultant to hire might be the PeopleSoft programmer. While there is still a shortage, the better programmers can become proficient with PeopleTools within a matter of weeks. They can master SQR and the other tools in short order as well. Hiring a programmer does not mean that you are hiring someone who is expert in the PeopleSoft application. Firms hiring coders will pay a pretty high rate for relatively little. On the one hand, if the programmers are part of a package included in a project management relationship, then they will be managed and led by the project manager and by the implementation partner. On the other hand, if the consultant is simply hired "à la carte," it is up to the project team to educate and manage this person. An inexperienced PeopleSoft programmer might modify or create programs that are less than optimal. These people have been placed at locations with varying degrees of success. The key is to hire an experienced person and to actively manage that person. The project team must treat this person as a basic programmer. Giving him or her any further leeway leaves the door open for major problems.

We have seen the different roles that PeopleSoft consultants, implementation partners, professional service technicians, and technical experts can fill. They can be a valuable cog in the wheel of the project team. Throwing additional resources at a project is often executive management's first reaction to a drawn-out timeline. Entire books have been written on the impact of additional resources to a project. Many of the results of such a decision are negative. It is far better to plan the use of consultants at the outset of the project. These resources have to be carefully selected and actively managed, if they are to provide the positive impact for which they are intended.

5.2 Selecting implementation partners and consultants

Selecting the company and the consultants is a critical task. Since the market is growing so fast, a major segment of the consultants in the business are inexperienced. Even the most experienced PeopleSoft Financials consultant cannot have more than a few years' experience, since the applications were only released in early 1993. The first thing organizations must do is to evaluate their implementation "vision." Whether it is a fast, vanilla implementation of only a few modules or a big-bang implementation of all modules at once, the organization must first establish what the goals are. This ought to be done anyway. It serves the purpose of forcing executive management to stick their necks out and give the project team some marching orders. Once that has been completed, then the organization can contact the PeopleSoft implementation partners and consulting firms to determine which one fits best with the vision strategy.

The organization should contact the implementation partner firms and obtain as much information about how they operate as possible. In addition, the organization should contact references—other organizations that have contracted with the partner firms. A detailed interview with a site reference can provide the most valuable insight. The organization should ascertain whether the firm completed its mission as contracted, and whether the consultants fit well within the context of the project. Communication channels and project processes should also be examined. What was the firm responsible for? Another valuable question is to ask both the firms and the site references what they consider their roles were not meant to be. This question from a divergent perspective can provide more insight into how the firm will fit in with the organization and the project team. The references should be asked specific questions whenever possible. General questions lead to vague answers. Before interviewing a site reference, the interviewer should prepare a carefully crafted list of questions designed to assess the consulting firm's ability to execute the job at hand and its fit within the organization. Without a formal list, the interviewer will fumble for discussion points and will leave the interview with more questions than answers. A well-conducted interview will yield most valuable insight into the effectiveness and fit of a particular consulting firm. Its importance cannot be underestimated, and the task should be given the most serious attention. Potential reference questions could include the following.

- Describe the philosophy or approach used by Company X. Also describe its impact on the organization, including political ramifications.

- Discuss the technical expertise of the consultants. To what degree did they have a command of the PeopleSoft environment?

- Discuss the functional expertise of the consultants. Be sure to include both the depth and breadth of it.

- Detail any processes that Company X and the consultants used to help ensure a smooth and appropriate transfer of knowledge to the organization.

- Describe your overall satisfaction with Company X.

- What did the consultants do well? What did they do not so well?

- Would you hire Company X and these consultants again?

- Offer any suggestions you might have for someone entering into a relationship with Company X.

- What must my organization do to prepare for and effectively work with Company X?

The organization should also thoroughly interview the consulting firm as to the number and types of projects in which it has been involved. Just because Company X has 12 implementations under its belt does not mean that any of those projects resembles the one facing it. The number of projects that the firm has completed is important because it does measure, to some degree, its endurance, and it reflects a level of expertise. Simply working on multiple iterations of the same type of project, contacting the same PeopleSoft technical support staff, and reading the same manuals over and over will cement the paradigm of the PeopleSoft applications and the project. It will be most insightful to scrutinize a past project that closely resembles the organization's project.

Among the factors to ignore when selecting an implementation partner are costs and immediate availability. The organization must plan, in advance, the role of the consulting firm in the project. That way, it will have ample time to establish a relationship with a particular firm. Without the planning, it is certain that the organization will be stuck paying higher rates and/or settling for a less-optimal fit with an inferior partnering firm. The cost should also be weighed carefully. In this arena, one truly does get what one pays for. Some consultants costing over $200 per hour provide much greater value than a lower-priced consultant. Just as computer hardware is measured in terms of price/performance ratio, the consultant should be measured on a price/productivity basis. The right consultant can be the star that the project team needs to guide it successfully. With careful planning, enough time, and a thorough review of potential consulting firms, the organization can establish a relationship with a partnering firm that can help the staffs through the life of the PeopleSoft project.

The following factors should be considered when selecting an implementation partner.

- Implementation philosophy or "vision"
- Level of PeopleSoft expertise and experience
- Past successes
- References

5.3 Implications to the project team

Hiring an outside consultant or implementation partner will have a significant impact on the day-to-day operation of the organization, the project team, and the project itself. There is no surer way to waste money than to have a poorly utilized and highly paid consultant on the company's dole. The consultants should be treated like prima donnas. They should be coddled. Anything they need, within reason of course, should be given to them. Assuming they are the right consultants for the job, with the right tools they will be amazingly productive. Let's examine some of the implications to the project team.

First and foremost, the project team has to be prepared for the consultants. Depending on the type of relationship and the amount of responsibility borne by the consulting firm, this can be either an intense task of short duration or it can be a less-intense process to support the work that the implementation partner will perform. In cases where the consultants are coming in to help with specific tasks, it might take the team several days or even a couple of weeks to properly prepare for their arrival. If they are to jump quickly into tasks, those tasks will have to be carefully, thoroughly, and formally defined on paper. The staff must also be available to answer questions and remove obstacles to the consultants' productivity. The team cannot overlook the logistical requirements of the consultants either. They will need a workstation, network connection, security access, workspace, storage shelves, and so forth. The consultants should provide a list of the accesses and work-area requirements. Most, if not all, of the consultants will bring their own notebook computer. They will probably need a workstation connected to the network, so they will need room for two computers and room for manuals and papers.

The organization should strive to arrange the schedules of its people around those of the consultants. They often will work only four-day weeks, perhaps Monday through Thursday each week. That gives the project team one day each week to go through the administrative tasks, which will no doubt pile up each week. Meeting schedules should reflect the work habits of the consultants. It is possible that the consultants will be crossing one or more time zones. The meetings should be scheduled at times when the consultants are most alert. Additionally, their workday may exceed that of some of the project team members. Usually they will strive to achieve 40 hours each week in four days. That makes for ten-hour workdays. Security and building access must take this into consideration. Also, production computing schedules might have to change to accommodate the schedule. Database backups might conflict with the development schedules of the consultants and might have to change. Keep in mind that the consultants are working away from home, likely in a strange town. Anything that can make their lives more comfortable will pay dividends for the project team. It is also appropriate for long-term contracts to include the consultants in social events or dinners after work. If the project team can establish a rapport with the consultants, then the team will have a resource from which to tap even beyond the scope of the consultants' formal involvement with the organization.

There are a few additional things to think about when managing consultants. One issue is the paperwork. Often they will bill regularly for expenses. Someone in the organization will need to manage this paperwork. Again, keeping the consultants happy is important. They will also need ready access to a phone. If they happen to get stuck due to weather, then the project team members or the organization should make accommodations where appropriate. There is a personal relationship dynamic, which is different for each person in each organization and each consultant. The rule of thumb is to make sure that the consultants are taken care of to a mutually acceptable level. They will be working closely with the project team, and if there is a good rapport between the group, it will be reflected in the productivity level. In any case, the consultants are a group of people who must be actively managed. If this is done effectively, then a mutually beneficial relationship can be developed and can provide a major benefit to the organization.

There are additional factors involved in hiring a consulting firm that are beyond the scope of this book. Items such as contract negotiation, noncompete requirements, nondisclosure requirements, and other issues can be researched and must receive appropriate attention. Selecting a PeopleSoft implementation partner is not a no-brainer. Partners come in many different "flavors." It is crucial for an organization to select one whose product/project vision closely matches its own. Many consulting firms will claim, "We do PeopleSoft," but they have precious little experience and perhaps no successes. It is crucial for those negotiating with potential partners to thoroughly examine their histories and contact multiple reference sites. At no time should the billing rate be a major consideration. Another specious argument sometimes used to justify hiring an implementation partner is "because we don't have the resources." On the one hand, it is valid because it should streamline the implementation and minimize wasted time and effort. On the other hand, these companies will require a specific level of involvement on the part of the implementation team and the organization as a whole. It is unlikely that, during the actual implementation project, the organization can cut the size of the team by hiring an implementation partner. Because the organization must support the software for the long haul, these firms, if they are to be successful, must transfer knowledge and expertise to the organization. They cannot do so without the appropriate staff allocated to the project.

Once the project strategy is defined and communicated and appropriate third-party help is on board, the implementation can begin. With a functional project team, a basic, communicated project plan, and procedures in place to monitor progress, the organization can focus on the next order of business: installing the software and determining the implementation options.

chapter 6

Installation

Okay, so the grueling selection process is complete. The organization has settled on PeopleSoft Financials and negotiated and signed the contracts. The project team is identified and now everyone is expecting miracles. The next step is to install the software. For some organizations installation will be a snap. For others it will be an event full of trial and error and a time of concentrated learning. In organizations that have an established local area network and database management system, as well as production control staff and operations staff, installing PeopleSoft will be a matter of technology and mechanics. Those who are perhaps less than leading-edge in their computing infrastructure will face considerable work to build the foundation for the PeopleSoft client/server software suite. For the purpose of educating the reader on the various aspects of the installation process, we will assume that there is little formal computing infrastructure available and that we must build it before the PeopleSoft installation team arrives on site.

6.1 Installation prerequisites

The first step in defining the requirements for the organization's infrastructure is to officially adopt the appropriate workstation configurations, network protocols, database management system, and file server operating system. PeopleSoft will run on a variety of platforms, and organizations can mix and match the individual client/server segments. There are literally dozens of potential operating environments under which PeopleSoft Financials might run. PeopleSoft Financials, as of version 5.1, runs on the following database management systems.

- DB2/MVS
- DB2/UNIX
- Informix
- Microsoft SQL Server
- Oracle
- SQLBase
- Sybase

Suppose an organization decided on ORACLE as its corporate database platform—at least for the PeopleSoft applications. Then, a decision must be made regarding which hardware and operating system platform the ORACLE database will run on. We now have numerous platforms and systems supported by PeopleSoft, and they change with each application release (see Table 6.1).

Now suppose that the client workstations will communicate with the ORACLE database server via the TCP/IP networking protocol. There are over 25 potential TCP/IP network driver vendors from which we can select. It is obvious that the sheer number of possibilities dictates that an organization must select its infrastructure based on sound business and technical justifications. Each option carries with it various costs and benefits. If an organization does not possess the knowledge necessary to make an informed decision, it should seek the guidance of PeopleSoft and, more appropriately, networking consultants. One key point for organizations that have no formal policies with respect to its technical infrastructure: It would be wise to consider adopting software and hardware platforms that are well supported by PeopleSoft. In other words, if PeopleSoft has a single NCR 3000 customer and 50 IBM RS/6000 customers, it is more likely that the software will enjoy long-term stability on the RS/6000 than on the NCR 3000 platform. For that reason, all organizations should seek a customer profile summary from PeopleSoft to determine how well PeopleSoft's customer base and experience can be put to use at their installation site. Now, let's examine the individual components of the infrastructure and what is required before PeopleSoft can schedule an installation date.

Table 6.1 Hardware platforms and operating systems supported by PeopleSoft

Hardware Platform	Operating System
Data General AviiON	DG/UX v5.4 R3.10
DEC Alpha	Open VMS 6.1 Digital UNIX 3.2
DEC VAX	VMS 5.5
HP 9000 8xx	HP-UX 9.04 HP-UX 10.01
IBM RS/6000	AIX 3.2.5 AIX 4.1.3
Intel PC	Windows NT 3.51 SCO UNIX <v3.2
NCR 3000	UNIX 5.4.0.3.0
Sun	Solaris 2.4

6.1.1 Workstations

The organization must procure and install appropriate, Intel-based personal computers. It is common for some organizations to clamor that it must be able to run PeopleSoft Financials on Macintosh computers. While this is technically feasible in some cases, using Microsoft Windows emulation products, for all but a few users it is not a practical option. Until PeopleSoft ports its toolset to the Macintosh operation system, organizations should insist that PeopleSoft users have Intel-based computers on their desks.

The actual configuration of the workstation is subject to organizational and budget constraints, but should be as powerful as the organization can justify. For version 5, PeopleSoft recommends no less than a 66 MHz, 486-based computer with a minimum of 8 MB of memory. That is a minimal configuration. In actual practice, a Pentium with 16 MB of RAM and 100 MHz clock speed or greater is desirable. As time passes, the price/performance curve for personal computers shifts toward the high end. The key is to buy the right workstation at the right time. It is a good idea to update the PeopleSoft workstation procurement set every three months to compensate for this shift. Large and fast hard drives of 1 GB or more will give the greatest flexibility to the system administrators when they install and upgrade PeopleSoft. At least one CD-ROM drive is required, and the workstations should have VGA controllers capable of displaying 640 x 480 resolution, although many end users would rather have higher resolution. Keep in mind that some end users will stare at the computer screen every day for most of the day. Providing 17" monitors to those people is certain to reduce eye strain and tension associated with computer screens. It can also be helpful to those creating reports and to developers, since they can view more on the screen at one time. Many purchasing agents balk at the expense of the monitor, but comparing the additional $400 for a larger monitor against the cost of a $40,000 employee being unproductive due to sickness and/or stress is really money well spent.

The workstation's operating system must be Microsoft Windows. That is currently available in three flavors: DOS/Windows 3.1, Windows 95, and Windows NT. Only if it is completely unavoidable should a PeopleSoft customer install new Windows 3.1 workstations. Beginning with version 6, PeopleSoft will require a 32-bit workstation operating system. The choice between Windows 95 and Windows NT is an organizational one and is not clear-cut. Often, organizations will install a mix of operating systems. If that is the case, it must be made clear that workstation support, training, and testing requires twice as much expertise, which means greater expense.

The networking components required on the workstation include a network interface card and appropriate network drivers. Ethernet and Token Ring are two common interface cards, but there are others. The network software drivers must be capable of transporting the database communication traffic between the workstation and the client and the network traffic to the file server.

6.1.2 Network

The subject of networks is a book in itself and is only tangentially related to this book's topic. That caveat aside, organizations should seek to install and run the fastest network they can justifiably afford. Speeds can range from a 4 MBPS token-ring network to 100 MBPS Ethernet and beyond. Each organization will have its own wiring and traffic protocols. As long as it can support the database communication between the client workstation and the database server hardware and has adequate printer support, any of the protocols supported by PeopleSoft will work. One point to remember though: The emergence of the World Wide Web, Internet, and "intranets" has brought TCP/IP to the forefront. In order to take advantage of the next wave of software capabilities, organizations should position themselves by ensuring that their networks are scalable and support the TCP/IP protocol. It must also be a protocol that the organization can support with its own staff. This may mean sending key individuals to additional training or hiring the expertise. So, in summary, the network must be stable, secure, supportable, capable of carrying the database traffic, and it must be supported by PeopleSoft.

6.1.3 File server

The file server is an often-neglected piece of the PeopleSoft installation process. In fact, in early releases, PeopleSoft recommended installing all software on the client workstations. Of course, network administrators know that it takes more effort to support that type of configuration when compared to one that has much of the software loaded and configured on a single, central, network file server. PeopleSoft Financials is compatible with virtually any file server that can communicate with the workstation, once the workstation is properly configured for PeopleSoft and the database management system. The file server needs a large amount of free disk space to house the application. For a file server that will only run a single version of the software, a minimum of 500 MB is needed. For a file server that will be used by developers to house more than one version of PeopleSoft—such as during the application upgrade—the server should have far more than this. Truthfully, to support the installation process, a minimum of 2 GB of available file server hard disk capacity is required. Tasks such as data conversion and customization require that the developers can freely access appropriate quantities of disk space. Failure to provide enough will hamper the developers' efforts.

6.1.4 Database server

The database server must be sized and configured to hold the relational database management system, multiple copies of the database, and other server software pieces. It has to be able to communicate with the workstations using the chosen network and database protocols. This is an entirely installation-specific process and will not be covered here, but some issues are important to discuss. First, the server machine must have adequate memory. It might be difficult to determine memory requirements from the outset, particularly if it is a new operating system and hardware platform for the organization. The installation team should seek the guidance of PeopleSoft and of its database management system vendor to determine how much memory to install initially, and it should be expandable in case experience indicates a need for additional memory. The second aspect to consider is disk storage capacity. One error made by organizations unfamiliar with PeopleSoft is to estimate the size of the production database and then multiply that by two in order to allow for a test copy. Implementations can typically require five or more copies of the database to ensure the integrity of the process. Often, a demo version of the database is used as a base, never-modified system for the developers. End users will likely want a "customized demo" version of the database where they can experiment and conduct training sessions. The developers will need both a test database and a production database and possibly more to appropriately code and test interfaces and customizations. And, depending on the structure of the project, other departments may want an additional copy of the database where they can experiment without affecting others.

The relational database management system that runs on the file server must be properly installed and configured, along with the appropriate software layers to allow it to communicate with the client workstations. Generally, it is desirable to have two copies of the database system—one for the production databases and one for the test databases. In addition to the database software, the server should have a COBOL compiler, C compiler, and SQR installed and functioning as well. Other software requirements will vary with the organization, but should also be installed and functional.

6.1.5 Printers

The printing capabilities of the PeopleSoft applications are excellent in some areas and limited in others. PeopleTools printing, for the most part, uses Microsoft Windows printer drivers. This is not completely true, since certain printing functions from within PeopleSoft actually generate "print files" in HP PCL format that must be manually sent to a printer. The reports that take advantage of Crystal Reports or nVision will work with most any Windows-capable printer. SQR reports generate HP PCL printer files with embedded printer commands. Given the variety of printing scenerios, it is best to settle on printers with the following capabilities.

- Sufficient speed as dictated by the organization—typically greater than ten pages per minute
- Network-ready interface card compatible with the file server's operating system to facilitate printer sharing and ease installation and support burdens
- Adequate memory to print pages with graphics usually 1.5 MB or greater—although more is probably better
- Support for "Hewlett-Packard's Page Control Language," or PCL, printer language
- TrueType font support

Aside from these capabilities, the project team will need to assess the proper quantity of printers and their locations. It is beneficial to establish a baseline "PeopleSoft" printer and urge end users to purchase that model. It will ease the support burden and facilitate information sharing if all departments use the same type of printer—for example, the organization may decide on the HP 5 line of laser printers to be used as PeopleSoft printers.

6.1.6 Installation team

The installation team may be completely different from the *implementation* team. Before an organization can schedule an installation date with PeopleSoft, it must identify the installation team members and make sure they are properly trained, having reviewed the *PeopleSoft Installation Guide* and the product release notes. The installation team members must also commit to total dedication to the installation process until it is

Table 6.2 Responsibilities of installation team members

Role	Responsibility
Database Administrator (DBA)	Reviews the database objects for conformance to standards. Typically sizes the table spaces, establishes authorizations, and is responsible for the ongoing reliability of the database system and the databases. Usually this person is required to create the databases.
LAN Administrator	Establishes permissions on the file server, installs the PeopleSoft applications on the server, and works with the workstation administrator to configure the workstations during network login. Often responsible for network printer support.
Workstation Administrator	Responsible for the installation of the workstation, including the database client communication software. Works closely with the LAN administrator to appropriately install required software on the workstation and file server.
Database Server System Administrator	Ensures network connectivity to the database server. Sets up the Process Scheduler on the server. Installs and compiles COBOL offline programs on the server machine.
PeopleSoft Administrator	Responsible for ongoing support of the PeopleSoft application itself, including creating operator classes and operators.

complete. Typically, installation should take between one and five days to complete and verify. Table 6.2 lists the responsibilities of the installation team members.

6.1.7 Preinstallation steps

The checklist shown in Table 6.3 represents the steps necessary to prepare the organization to install the base PeopleSoft application. Implementation should not be scheduled until these steps are completed and verified. The specifics of each step will be determined by the platforms adopted.

Table 6.3 Preinstallation steps

No.	Step	Team Members
1	Review the *Installation Guide* and release notes.	All
2	Review the updates and fixes available on PeopleSoft Forum.	All
3	Install the database management system (such as DB2 or ORACLE).	DBA

Table 6.3 Preinstallation steps

No.	Step	Team Members
4	Install the database communication software on the database server.	System Administrator, DBA
5	Establish appropriate disk space on the file server.	LAN Administrator
6	Install the database communication software on the workstation.	Workstation Administrator
7	Ensure that the workstation can communicate with the database via its communication software.	DBA, System Administrator, Workstation Administrator
8	Back up the database server.	DBA or System Administrator
9	Back up the file server.	LAN Administrator
10	Back up the workstation configuration.	Workstation Administrator

When the infrastructure is in place and the checklist is complete, the installation team is ready to install the PeopleSoft application itself.

6.2 *PeopleSoft installation*

PeopleSoft will schedule a date to install the software at the customer site. They are competent and lead the process well, which is not easy given the wide array of possible configurations. The major responsibility for the customer is to guarantee the complete attention of all members of the installation team. With some variation, the PeopleSoft installation expert will guide the installation team through the necessary steps to install and verify PeopleSoft Financials with a goal of transferring knowledge to the installation team.

6.2.1 *Set up the file server*

The first installation task is to load the software to the file server. People-Soft distributes its software on CD-ROM, so the installers must have access to either a workstation with a CD-ROM drive or a network CD-ROM drive. The actual setup process is much like installing a PC software package such as word processing. From the Windows run prompt, the installer simply runs PSSETUP.EXE. After answering a few questions about the installation drive and directory structure and selecting which products to install, the setup program will copy the software from the CD to the file server's hard drive. This location on the file server is the central location from which the other installation tasks are managed. The file server step is trivial and takes little time assuming the workstation and the file server are functioning properly on the network and that adequate disk space is available.

6.2.2 Set up the workstation

PeopleSoft delivers a methodology for setting up workstations. To install a workstation, the installer runs a workstation setup program, which is located on the file server. After filling in a few default values, the setup program will copy some files locally to the hard drive, create a specific DOS batch file, and modify the workstation's AUTOEXEC.BAT file. The specific DOS batch file created will be customized for the installation's database and network drive/directory structure. It contains numerous SET statements to set DOS environment variables required for the PeopleSoft application. It appears that PeopleSoft's entire workstation installation philosophy is designed to support a situation where one workstation accesses multiple PeopleSoft applications with differing database options. One batch file may be named PSORA.BAT for ORACLE. Another may be named PSDB2.BAT for DB2. When a given workstation must access multiple PeopleSoft configurations, simply rebooting and executing a different batch file is all that is required. However, this procedure is a little confusing for novice users and provides unnecessary flexibility for the workstations in most organizations.

The workstation installation really comes down to creating the correct environment to enable the PeopleSoft application to run. The delivered methodology is a good starting point, but organizations with existing local area network standards and software distribution and installation methods may wish to modify it to more closely match their own. When a workstation logs into the file server, the following steps must be performed.

- Modify the DOS path to include entries for PeopleTools and other third-party products such as Crystal Reports and the database communication drivers. For NetWare, the login script may include entries such as:

```
Map Root G:=dpsrvr2/dpapps:
Map s3:=g:\fs501\bin
Map s4:=g:\fs501\crw
```

```
Map s5:=g:\orawin\bin
Map s6:=g:\fs501\sqrbinw
```

- Set the appropriate DOS environment variables. PeopleSoft requires between 20 and 30 environment variables, such as:

```
SET COBDIR=G:\FS501\CBLBIN
SET SQRBIN=G:\FS501\SQRBINW
```

- Install and ensure access to any third-party packages such as Microsoft Excel and Crystal Reports. Again, the software can be installed either on the workstation or on the file server as long as the workstation has access to it.

- Create icons for the appropriate program executables, so the workstation will have a means to invoke PeopleSoft.

The installation team must carry out this installation process for every workstation that will access PeopleSoft. The network administrator and the workstation administrator, working together, can create an installation configuration and process that is most efficient for its network. It is wise, however, to completely install a single workstation using PeopleSoft's format. Then, using that installation as a starting piont, they will be able to formulate their own process.

6.2.3 Create databases

The next step in the process is to actually create a PeopleSoft database. The installation team will need to learn this process thoroughly because every time the team installs a new database, it must follow these steps. Creating a PeopleSoft database means to create either a Demo database or a SYS database, which is complete and is distributed by PeopleSoft. The SYS database is a complete application including all tables, panels, reports, queries, and other objects, but with no data. It contains only the default, PeopleSoft chart field tables, Account, DeptID, Product, ProjectID, and so forth. The data tables are not populated. In other words, the journal and ledger tables are empty, the chart field tables have no values in them, and so on. The Demo database is a SYS database with demonstration data included. Most organizations install a copy of a Demo database for comparison purposes. The SYS database is used as the starting point for the organization's implementation, and typically more than one copy of a SYS database is required for the implementation. The process itself is fairly mindless if the installer follows PeopleSoft's instructions.

1 Create the database script. This is accomplished using a PeopleSoft utility. The installer specifies which products, the name of the database, the database Access ID and Access Password, and selects either the Demo or the SYS database option. Then, pressing the Create Scripts button generates the various files needed to install the database.

2 Transfer the database scripts to the database server.

3 Create the database on the server using the script. At this point it will be empty.

4 Create the various tables and authorizations required to connect to the database. Again, these steps are detailed in the *PeopleSoft Installation Guide*.

5 Run the Data Mover scripts generated in step 1. To do this, the installer signs onto the database from a workstation using the PeopleTools Data Mover utility and executes the script. This will create the database structures and populate the appropriate tables.

6 Run certain utilities to clean up and audit the database. These are specified by PeopleSoft.

7 Create all of the database views. This is accomplished either via Data Mover or via the Data Designer.

8 Load the COBOL SQL statements into the database. The PeopleSoft COBOL programs retrieve their SQL statements from a table, and this step loads that table.

9 Define an operator to access the database.

10 Run appropriate acceptance testing processes.

6.2.4 Set up the batch COBOL and Process Schedulers

We won't discuss the specific step required to set up the COBOL programs and the job execution scheduler, Process Scheduler. Most software developers are familiar enough with loading and compiling programs that following the steps in the book will be easy. As long as the database server has the appropriate COBOL compiler and C compiler, no problems should occur.

Once these installation steps are completed, the Demo and SYS databases can be used by workstations that are properly configured. The only task left is to configure additional workstations for all members of the implementation team and others who will need immediate access. Assuming that no major problems are encountered by the installation team, the installation should be completed within one week. Be certain that the installation team carefully takes notes and questions the PeopleSoft installation professional, since new releases of the software will require similar steps to install. Careful documentation during this initial release will benefit the organization for future upgrades and database installations. In addition, if the implementation team has a single person capable of bridging all areas, from the workstation and file server to the database server, it can be a huge help in performance tuning and trouble-shooting. The installation is tricky, because it involves so many layers of software and spans multiple hardware platforms. If the installation team is thorough and methodical, however, the installation won't be too painful and the team members will learn a great deal about the PeopleSoft configuration process.

6.3 Remote access

There is one more issue that is important to discuss, and that is remote access. Remote access provides a means for a PeopleSoft workstation to communicate with the database from a remote location. There are several configurations available for remote access (see Figure 6.1). Depending on the level of use and the performance requirements and other issues, the organization will need to choose the method with the best fit. PeopleSoft has business partners who can provide secure, managed remote access server configuration.

Many organizations wait until after PeopleSoft is in production before they tackle the remote access issue. This is not an ideal situation for the implementation team. The team members will probably have some weeks during which they will work an excessive number of hours, perhaps as high as 80. This can put tremendous strain on them and their families. By providing a means for them to telecommute, some of the additional hours can be logged from home. Be clear, however, that the remote access is not a substitute for on-site hours. The team will need to be in close and constant communication which cannot be easily accomplished from remote locations. Telecommuting will offer team members a

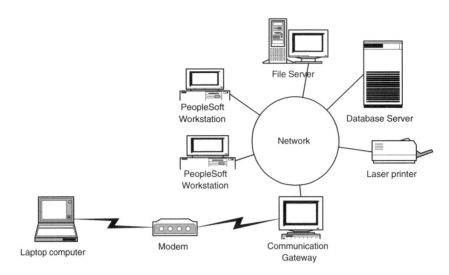

Figure 6.1 PeopleSoft remote configuration

degree of flexibility, however, and ease the burden that the rigors of the project will place on them.

In some cases, the deployment strategy will dictate that some production users of the PeopleSoft application be located remotely from the installation. In this situation, users may access PeopleSoft from a remote location to enter their own general ledger journal entries, purchase orders, and payables vouchers, or to generate their own nVision reports. When the organization has remote users who frequently access the system, it is imperative that the implementation team consider the remote access issue as part of the project. There are several vendors with well-performing products that can meet this need. Other, less-expensive solutions can be employed, but won't enjoy the same level of performance, security, and fault tolerance. A site visit to a PeopleSoft customer with a remote access configuration can be helpful. Be certain that these remote production users are not neglected. The implementation team needs them as their allies, too, since they will represent the software and project at those locations. Whatever the remote access needs are, the team will have several alternatives. One is certain to fit well within requirements and budget constraints.

chapter 7

Implementation options

After the installation team has successfully installed PeopleSoft Financials, it is time for the real work to begin. The implementation team must successfully match the software to the organization and identify areas where the software does not meet its needs. At the same time, the team must define and enter the myriad parameters that drive the application software. It will have to adopt and code an appropriate chart field configuration, establish security authorizations, and menu structures. At the same time, the developers on the team will create specifications for software customization, which they can estimate and schedule for coding. This is a lot to accomplish and may take between two and six months or more, depending on the combination of financial applications being installed.

The entire team should work together in focused sessions to painstakingly determine all of the software's options. It must also identify major business procedure changes and set them in motion. In order to properly and effectively carry out the meetings, the team needs a meeting location, which should be comfortable and have ample room and table space to spread out materials. An overhead projector capable of projecting a computer screen image is a necessity. In the absence of such a device, the room's computer should have a monitor of at least 17 inches. The members of the team will also appreciate whiteboards, refreshments, and privacy. They will spend many long days in the room and poor facilities will quickly wear on them.

Accommodations for the "PeopleSoft Command Central" should include the following.

- A powerful, PeopleSoft workstation
- Flow-charting software
- A network connection for the workstation
- Ample room to accommodate the team
- Adequate table space for the team members to spread out manuals and papers
- Comfortable seating
- Sufficient lighting
- An overhead projector
- Computer screen projecting equipment
- Access to restrooms and refreshments
- Whiteboards

Assuming the staff is formally assigned and the "command" room is identified and appropriately stocked, the team then needs a road map to guide it through the system definition process. We'll label this process "prototyping." The prototyping process provides structure to the product and process analysis undertakings and begins with some level of business process reengineering.

7.1 Business process reengineering and PeopleSoft

Business process reengineering (BPR) is basically the process whereby a unit's procedures, workflow processes, and business rules are examined in the light of today's business climate and corporate culture. The output of the reengineering process should be a new set of processes, procedures, business rules, and workflows that are most efficient and closely aligned with the organization's goals as well as the particular unit's goals. That is a short description of a difficult and time-consuming process. In the best of circumstances, PeopleSoft Financials is being installed as a result of BPR. In the worst case, it is being installed without regard to the underlying business rules, workflows, and process requirements. While it is beyond the scope of this book to study BPR in depth, a discussion of some terms, benefits, and implications for the implementation project is warranted. Let's begin by breaking down some of the terms associated with business processes in general.

7.1.1 Business rules

Business rules are rigid requirements by which the organization is compelled to abide. A sample business rule might be: Employees may purchase company stock through a company sponsored plan at not less than 85 percent of the fair market price of the stock on the day of purchase. Reasons for business rules are numerous, but include: federal or local governmental regulations, generally accepted accounting principles, requirements from internal and external customers, environmental constraints, and so on. Organizations may have relatively little control over the business rules. Changing business rules is usually difficult and may require significant negotiation between the parties involved. The most discomforting characteristic of a business rule is that it may be subject to change at any time and without prior notification. An individual department may have business rules that are established by the organization. In this case, savvy managers may use the PeopleSoft implementation as an opportunity to justify modifying their business rules to their advantage.

7.1.2 Policies

Policies differ from business rules in that they are established voluntarily. Typically, a department has control over its own policies; although the line between a business rule and a policy is not a clear one. A sample policy might be: All accounts payable checks over $25,000 must be approved by the Vice President of Finance. Policies are frequently outdated. Policies put into place ten years ago may have little or no relevance or merit in today's business climate.

7.1.3 Process

A process is simply a business procedure. A process begins with an input, which is followed by a series of decisions, operations, inspections, storage, and/or rework steps. The end result of a process is an output, which is quite often an input into another process or the process of an internal or external customer. Since the quality of inputs directly affects the quality of outputs, improving processes, which in turn improves the quality of their outputs, can have a cascadingly positive impact for an organization and its suppliers and customers.

7.1.4 Workflow

Workflow can be defined in a number of ways. Workflow-enabled software has been a highly visible market segment in recent years. In our case, we'll define workflow as the physical implementation of a process. A given workflow might only be part of a process or it might span multiple processes.

7.2 Why reengineer?

The implementation of PeopleSoft Financials is possibly the best opportunity an organization will ever have to reengineer its business processes. It is an arduous task, however, and some employees may be so anxious to use the new software that they will neglect this all-important step. In fact, executive management in many organizations may not even be aware of the state of their business processes. To them, it may be common sense that departments and the organization as a whole should examine and modify their practices consistently over time. The truth is, however, that most organizations are too busy keeping pace and focusing on other pressures to invest that much time and effort into their own infrastructure. So let's look at some justification factors that the project team can present to executive management to sanction a solid BPR effort in conjunction with the PeopleSoft implementation.

7.2.1 Project buy-in

Undertaking BPR will require that the project team include the staff involved in the processes being reengineered. Their expertise and experience in the organization is vital to properly analyze the needs of the organization and the history behind the various business rules, policies, and processes currently being used. If these individuals are part of the process and, actually, part of the solution, they will be more apt to support the project team and champion the new software. Since supporters, at first, will be few and far between, any opportunity to gain additional ones is worth the effort.

7.2.2 Maximize the software's fit

We assume that PeopleSoft Financials will do a fairly decent job of meeting the organization's requirements, but that is not always the case. Sometimes major software purchases are not made for the right reasons. Implementation teams may be asked to install software that does not really fit well in the organization under existing business rules and policies. Much of the software's functionality may not be applicable and ends up unused. By modifying the business processes and policies to work within the context of PeopleSoft Financials, the organization can take the most advantage of its new software, maximizing the return on investment and providing the most benefit to its departments, customers, and suppliers.

7.2.3 Minimize software support costs

Buy-in and software fit are rather indirect reasons to justify the time, effort, and organizational upheaval common in BPR. Executive management may find it easy to ignore advice and proceed without it. They will find it more difficult to ignore the bottom-line cost associated with major system customization and recurring upgrade costs. When business rules and policies are not supported directly by PeopleSoft Financials' base functionality, the developers are forced to bridge this "fit-gap" with customizations. This is expensive and time-consuming. The more customizations that are required before production, the longer the implementation will take. Once the software is in production, the subsequent, regular upgrade process will involve reapplying these modifications again and again. By setting the vision of the executive management for a vanilla software package, which is easy to support and upgrade (freeing developers to work on other projects), the project team may be able to persuade the organization to commit to a business process reengineering phase in the project.

7.3 Obstacles to reengineering

Reengineering efforts are not normally embraced by everyone in an organization. Some organizations' BPR efforts even fail, because their environments are not conducive to the major operational changes. Reality dictates that the project team examine the obstacles facing them before embarking on the trip to new and improved business processes. It is pointless to waste time if the organization is not receptive to the changes from the beginning. On the other hand, many obstacles can be avoided if they are identified from the beginning.

7.3.1 Process owners

Many processes, however senseless, are meticulously nurtured by some person or group having a vested interest in its perpetuity. Often these "process owners" are deeply entrenched in the organization's power structure, making it difficult to sidestep them by challenging the processes at a different organizational level. These people may even have authored the processes to begin with. In that case, the project team is faced with a champion of an inefficient process, who will go to the mat to defend it. To overcome these ingrained processes and their staunch supporters, the project team must structure the new process in such a way that it can be the owner of this new process. If the supporters are led to believe that they are the force behind the changes, then they will be supporters of the new processes and an ally of the project team.

7.3.2 "If it ain't broke"

Unfortunately, "broke" is a relative and subjective term. A process may work well for some and not well for others. Or it may be a question of a process working well or one working even better. Changing the way an organization operates must be justified on the basis of cost/benefit. Just because a given process or procedure is effective, does not mean that it is optimal. Again, if the BPR effort includes those involved in the process itself, they will gain a vested interest in the new process and support the implementation of PeopleSoft Financials in their areas.

7.3.3 Fear of change

Many people, for a variety of reasons, resist change of any kind. Some people do not naturally and readily assimilate change in their lives and that translates to their workplace as well. This is not a negative in and of itself—for instance, in the Department of Defense, resistance to change by the software developers is probably perceived as a desirable trait, given the potential for disaster the smallest error carries with it. In other lines of work, however, resistance to change can be devastating, particularly as the world makes the transformation from the Industrial Age to the Information Age. Change is running rampant throughout organizations. Corporations are downsizing, merging, growing, starting, dying. Inside the organizations, departments are facing greater pressures than at any time in their history. They are being told to do more with less, improve quality, empower workers, collaborate, and assume greater responsibility. The massive change rate prevalent in today's business climate can be overwhelming. Adding BPR on top of the existing rate of change may just break the camel's back. However, if it is properly framed, the reengineering can be a light at the end of the tunnel. It can be the vehicle by which the department or organization is saved from the onslaught of the Information Age. By focusing on the benefits of efficiency gains and improved quality inherent in BPR efforts, the project team can convince many change-resistant people to join the effort. In other cases, due largely to personality traits and organizational history, the team will simply have to dictate the new processes until the benefits are evident enough that the skeptics become supporters.

7.3.4 Lack of clout

When the implementation team sets out to change the way parts of the organization do business, it should be certain that it has enough muster to carry out the effort. Nothing will stall the effort like a team without any real influence. This is why the structure of the implementation team itself is so important. The team must have the power to make decisions and the credibility to assume the support of executive management. If the team is seen as weak, or it does a poor job of marketing and carrying out BPR, it may be undermined by more powerful line managers or executive managers. The organization should realistically assess the implementation team's influence and be sure that it will measure up to the task at hand.

7.3.5 Lack of abilities

While this reason is so obvious it seems pointless to discuss it, it may be more subtle and more common than one may realize. The world is *not* full of experienced process analyzers and developers. It is not necessarily a trait automatically carried by programmers. The PeopleSoft project may represent an organization's first attempt at streamlining its business operations, and the team may not know where to start. In this case, it is a good idea to enlist the help of an outside consultant to assist in the reengineering tasks. Or, if the organization has faith in the team's talent, it may opt to provide some training in BPR to the team, so that it will have the expertise to effectively carry out the effort.

Whatever the mix of people and processes in an organization, business process reengineering, when done appropriately, will render tangible, cost-justified benefits. There are a variety of reasons why it might get sidetracked, but all are avoidable in most cases. Firms that have adopted an effective Total Quality Management (TQM) mentality will probably find their staffs open and receptive to these efforts. Other firms might find pockets of enthusiasm sprinkled throughout the organization that can be used as a springboard to start the effort. Hopefully, the financial areas will be ready and willing to examine their processes in light of PeopleSoft Financials and strive to attain the most efficient processes which effectively fit within the PeopleSoft paradigm.

7.4 Model the current business processes

The first milestone for the prototyping phase of the implementation is for the project team to model the organization's current business processes. Using flow-charting software and the overhead projector, the group should identify the major business processes contained in the departments that will be using PeopleSoft. The most efficient means for doing this is to create traditional Total Quality Management process diagrams. This type of diagram is not represented graphically in the traditional sense. It is really a linear collection of steps, each identified by a symbol representing a step in the process. Next to the symbol is a thorough description of that step. (See Figure 7.1.)

The benefits of the business process diagram are many. First, it is easy to create in a group session. The diagrams that show process flows with arrows can be very tedious to build in a group setting and tend to

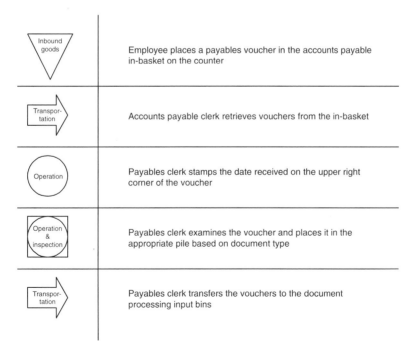

Figure 7.1 Sample business process diagram

slow down the process. The description section of the business process diagram offers space for a great deal of detail concerning the steps of the process and the business reasons behind them. It is also easy to identify areas of delay or storage, which are prime targets for efficiency gains. This type of diagram is also commonly used in many organizations as a tool for identifying processes in the TQM environment, and they may be readily available. If not, their familiarity ought to facilitate a short startup time for this process. This is not the only way to model the current business processes, but if the team has no experience with process modeling, it is an excellent choice.

The process descriptions themselves need to be as detailed as possible. It is easy for a group to give a five-minute description of a business process, but it will be of little value. To say, for example, that an employee places a payables voucher in the accounts payable in-basket, where it is collected and passed onto a payables clerk for processing, is to trivialize the process itself. The process might rather be as follows. The employee places a payables voucher in the accounts payable in-basket. The payables mail clerk retrieves all mail from the in-basket. The clerk transfers the mail to the sorting desk. He or she stamps each voucher with the date and then sorts them into three piles, depending on their type. The clerk then transfers the piles into the appropriate voucher-processing in-basket. Now this is a simplified description of the processes found in most organizations, but the reader can distinguish the difference in the level of detail between the two examples. The detail is critical, and the more that the team can include, the more useful this process modeling will be.

The major advantage of investing the time to do what some might consider a waste of time is to uncover business requirements, both hidden and overt. We use the term "business requirement" loosely, because some requirements may be simply policies or guidelines. At any rate, the detailed descriptions of each step will lead to in-depth discussions of why departments carry out particular steps. It is an illuminating procedure. These processes often carry with them decades of iterative policy changes and business rule adjustments, which are simply layered one upon the other. Often, the most chagrined team members are those who are currently carrying out redundant or unnecessary steps. On the other hand, the modeling process will also bring to light those steps that are justifiable. By drilling down to the detailed reason why, the underlying business requirements can be identified and documented.

The modeling process can effectively assist the team in analyzing current processes, eliminating inefficient and unjustified steps and identifying those business rules that must be followed when the new software is in production.

7.5 Establish chart fields

Perhaps no single decision will have as far-reaching effects as that of the organization's chart field configuration. The decision will touch literally every department—from the CEO down to the most remote niche employees in the organization. Chart fields basically represent the organizational and financial attributes by which the organization will report its financial information. Account is obviously a chart field in every case. It is a requirement to track financial transactions through the various asset, liability, income, and expense categories. Other potential chart fields are department, project, grant, product, and just about any other category. Government and public sector entities have some unique chart field requirements to support fund accounting. In many organizations, no single person can explain *why* the chart fields exist in their current form. Some may be able to define them, but nobody can explain, in concise terms, what exactly each chart field means and why they were chosen. Two common problems existing in many in-house developed financial systems are using a single chart field for more than one purpose and assigning meanings to subportions of an individual chart field.

When a chart field is used to represent more than one attribute, it can lead to a whole host of problems. Ideally, if a chart field is defined as **department,** it should mean only department. This means that each official department will own one and only one **department** chart field value. The rules that determine what constitutes a department are usually defined by the Human Resources. To adopt that definition is only common sense. However, many financial departments balk at this idea by saying "HR's departments are different from our departments." To say that is to miss the point. A department should have a single organizational definition. If the financial department does not match one for one to the HR department, in all likelihood, the financial department means more than "department." In some cases it might mean department and in other cases it might mean project or another discrete corporate attribute. By combining definitions into a single chart field, the work required to track and maintain that chart field is made needlessly complex. Now, getting an organization to define these business rules is a different issue. Politics will certainly be part of the equation, so those trying to orchestrate a chart field change must do so cautiously.

Also, in many in-house financial applications the tendency is to embed hierarchical structures within the values of a chart field—for example, the **Account** field might use the first position to identify whether it is a revenue account or an expense account. Further, it might use the second digit to identify, for revenue accounts, whether it is revenue from products or services. This kind of embedded logic is common in other chart fields, too. (See Figure 7.2.)

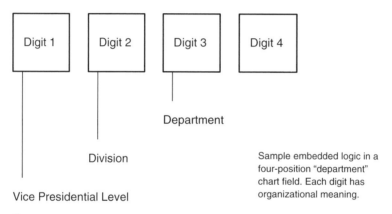

Figure 7.2 **Example of chart field with embedded logic**

This problem of embedded logic should be easier to sell than getting organizational units to agree on a single definition for each chart field. That is because by using PeopleSoft's Tree Manager, financial users can take the logic that once was built into the numbering scheme of the chart field and graphically represent it in a tree. It is functionally helpful to reserve ranges of values for specific tree nodes, but there is no restriction requiring it, so users can eliminate all definitional meanings of various digits of the fields.

The implementation team may or may not have the requisite experience to research and actualize a new set of chart fields. The process need not take excessive time. A week or two of concentrated effort and access to the appropriate information and staff is probably enough. Basically, to define chart fields one need only ask the question, "Given our strategic plans and goals, on what key attributes do we need to report our financial data?" Easy to say, but not easy to do. The team can hire consultants experienced in chart field definition to complete the process. They might have a better chance of garnering executive support than the team. If that is the case, the team must be sure it is completed as early in the implementation as possible.

7.5.1 Chart fields in PeopleSoft

In PeopleSoft Financials, each chart field stands on its own as a discrete segment. Together they comprise the chart fields, which uniquely identify individual entries in the general ledger. They ship the software with a chart field combination, which may work without modification for some installations. The chart fields are: Business Unit, Account, Department, Product, Project, and Statistics Code. Those unfamiliar with newer financial software may balk at so many chart fields, but in PeopleSoft Financials, the user only needs to enter those chart fields that apply—for example, money that the organization owns, which does not belong to a specific department, such as money in a checking account shared by all departments, is held only in that account. The other chart fields are left blank. If a department has a project underway, to identify transactions as related to that project, they simply enter the project ID in the Project ID chart field. When the Project ID is left blank, then the transaction does not relate to any project. When journal entries are posted to the general ledger, they are posted using all chart field values that are entered, making it easy to report on specific chart field values. This is a difficult concept for some to grasp. Getting them to see the paradigm is difficult, but essential to secure their support for a new structure. To understand how chart fields function, let's examine the following sample journal entries. For this example, we will ignore any offsetting entries.

Bus. Unit	Account	Department	Product	Project	Stat. Code	Amount
ATF	1011	1005				100
ATF	1011	1006	25			250
ATF	1011	1006	25			107
ATF	1011	1006	25			88
ATF	1011	1007		NCR1		125
ATF	1012	1007		NCR1		37

Bus. Unit	Account	Department	Product	Project	Stat. Code	Amount
ATF	1012	1007				100
ATF	1012	1007				50

When these journals are posted to the ledger, the posting process will add the amounts to the appropriate row in the ledger. Distinct ledger rows are identified by each unique combination of chart field values for each accounting period and ledger. Assuming these entries are all for the same accounting period and ledger and that no other transactions with these chart field combinations have been loaded to the ledger, the following ledger rows would be created during the post.

Bus. Unit	Account	Department	Product	Project	Stat. Code	Posted Total Amt.
ATF	1011	1005				$100
ATF	1011	1006	25			$445
ATF	1011	1007		NCR1		$125
ATF	1012	1007		NCR1		$37
ATF	1012	1007				$150

Now, when end users wish to report against the ledger, they can report against any combination of chart fields. To query the total value posted against project NCR1, they can simply select those rows with NCR1 project, yielding a total of $162. To report all activity affecting department 1007, they can query that value, which would retrieve $312 in our example. Further, when the reports are based on trees created using the Tree Manager, end users can base reports on the hiearchy of one or more chart fields. The tremendous flexibility of PeopleSoft reporting is seen in this design. To take advantage of it, however, the project team must identify an appropriate and logical chart field configuration.

We've examined the merits of a solid chart field configuration and briefly touched on the process used to define one. When this is complete, it is appropriate for the implementation team to apply the customization to the database that it will use for the product walk throughs. It is easier for the team members to understand the panels and reports if the chart fields are familiar. For an inexperienced developer, this will probably take a couple of weeks. PeopleSoft is designed to allow individual installations to customize chart fields. Its design faciliates the process, but it is still a manual process. For this reason, the team may decide to use existing chart fields for other purposes. They may, for example, use the Product field to represent an entirely different chart field, assuming Product is not part of their chart field configuration. In this case, the only work involved is to change the field labels on all panels and reports. Generally, the more drastic the chart field customization, the trickier it will be to apply. When the chart field customization is complete, the implementation team is ready to begin the detailed software walk-through sessions.

7.6 *Product review sessions*

When the implementation team has finished modeling the current business processes, assuming members have attended the appropriate training, it must forge ahead and figure out how to configure and customize PeopleSoft Financials so that it meets the organization's business requirements. Within this same process, all key business process, requirements, and procedures need to be evaluated and modified to be more efficient and to work within the software's framework. There are many ways the team can go about this, but a common and effective one is to hold product review, or "prototype," sessions. During these prototype sessions, the implementation team has to discuss every parameter, option, and process of the software. Together with the customizations made, this process will literally shape PeopleSoft Financials to fit the organization. The sessions provide a methodology to systematically evaluate the myriad decisions. Without a formal process such as this, it is exceedingly difficult to effectively set up the tables that drive PeopleSoft Financials and to determine how and where to customize it.

In order to arrive at the level of detail required by the prototyping process, the implementation team must focus its time and efforts exclusively on it. The single biggest mistake that a project team can make is to attempt to do this product review in only a couple of hours each day. The topics are so intertwined and complex, that, to be effective, the sessions must be long enough and often enough to provide continuity to the effort. Besides, it is time consuming and the project cannot go forward until it is complete. On the other hand, the team members will have certain unavoidable administrative tasks, which they will have no choice except to complete. The prototyping process should leave ample time for them to do these things without falling too far behind at any one time. A workable solution is to schedule all-day sessions, four days each week, leaving one day per week to address and eliminate distractions. Using the "command central" room, with all of its equipment and projection capabilities, the team can spend full days concentrating on how to set up and configure the software and how these decisions will affect the organization's business processes.

The exact timeframe that the prototyping sessions will cover is a function of many variables. First, it depends upon the scope of the implementation. If the team is prototyping only a single module, such as General Ledger, then it will take much less time than if it is trying to do all financial modules at once. The time for a single module can fluctuate, too, depending upon the level of expertise of the team members and the degree to which the base software meets the requirements. The team should plan to spend from three to six weeks per module prototyping. To implement General Ledger, Accounts Payable, and Purchasing, for instance, the prototyping phase would probably last between two and four months. This time further justifies not implementing all modules of PeopleSoft Financials at one time. If you add Fixed Assets, Project Costing, and Inventory, then the time expands to between four and eight months. This is only to determine how to implement the software. It ignores the interfaces, the customizations, and the data conversion. The team should choose no more modules than it can prototype in a reasonable period of time. The sessions are grueling, and the software must provide some tangible benefit in an acceptable time frame to keep executive management happy.

The actual prototyping sessions have to cover two basic areas of the software. PeopleSoft Financials first requires that all of its tables be set up prior to operating the software. The software's documentation includes a detailed guide explaining how to set up the tables. Data must be entered on various panels in a specific order. The first order of business in the prototyping sessions should be to discuss and define these table setup values in meticulous fashion. The discussion of each parameter will lead, if properly done, to its underlying business rules and policies. When discussing vendor payment terms in Accounts Payable, for example, the team must explicitly define the rules of how the payables department will deal with payment terms. What will be default payment terms for vendors who do not specify? Are there situations when discounts should be taken even when the discount due date has passed? Obviously, a single parameter might take six hours to formalize and document. Multiply that by the hundreds of parameter settings driving the software and it is easy to see why this is a laborious effort. Other items, such as SETID and Business Unit options, are much more complex and really drive the processing of the entire organization. They might take several meetings to resolve. Decisions will be made daily in the prototyping sessions, so we must reiterate that the implementation team has to include those who have the authority to make most of these decisions. The sessions build on one another, and when the team is forced to wait for approval of its decisions, it impedes the progress of future meetings.

When the parameters are defined and entered, the next step is to examine the processes built within the software and apply them to the organization—for instance, the chart field maintenance panels, say for **Department ID**, must be reviewed in detail. The team must define how each field will be used in the organization and who will and will not be allowed to update these fields. During this process, too, the team will need to examine how well the panels and processes match the organization's requirements. Where they fall short of critical requirements, the software has to be customized, enhanced, or extended. Whatever the terminology, the detailed specifications of all requirements have to be identified and documented during this process. The developers will use these specifications to estimate and code the changes to the base software. The exact order of topics for this portion is up to each implementation team. Two logical options are to follow the order presented in the training guides for the software or to follow the order presented in the PeopleSoft Financials documentation. Any other order may work as well, as long as it includes all panels and all processes. If the team is implementing more than one module simultaneously, it is a good idea to rotate modules by day—for example, the sessions might focus on General Ledger on Monday and Wednesday and Purchasing on Tuesday and Thursday.

Another subject for the review sessions is financial reporting. Reporting in PeopleSoft Financials is extremely powerful and flexible, but the "canned" reports are certainly not going to be adequate for any installation. The team must review all reports that are shipped and match them to the organization's reporting needs. Reports required by the organization that are not provided by PeopleSoft can be added to the customization list. The end result of all of these meetings should be as follows.

1 Documented business processes as they will exist after implementation

2 Detailed specifications of all required customizations

3 Security profiles for all panels and operators

4 Documented reporting requirements

5 Effective parameter setttings, which tailor the PeopleSoft Financials for the particular organization

The team may choose to include additional topics and issues in the prototyping sessions such as workflow and document imaging. However, each layer of complexity that is added will put the success of the project at greater risk. Depending upon the expertise and knowledge of the team and the organization, advanced features such as these can be included in a second phase, after the software is functioning in production.

In truth, the best way to ensure that this part of the implementation is successful is to hire a PeopleSoft implementation partner to do this. Each one will have its own unique way to go about this. By comparing the philosophy of each candidate implementation partner, the project team can select the one it feels will work best for its circumstances. If that is not an option, however, there are a few suggestions to follow. First, be sure that the timing of the prototyping sessions is not too long after the team members attend training. To send staff off to training only to wait six weeks to begin will increase the startup time for the prototype sessions as they reacquaint themselves with PeopleSoft. To conduct the meetings themselves, two individuals should be involved extensively. First, the project leader will probably lead the meetings. He or she should strive to keep the meetings on track, while still leaving some tangential room to ensure that issues are thoroughly discussed. That leader needs the support of a "scribe." The scribe is someone who runs the computer, takes the notes, and documents the decisions made during the meetings. The meeting leader cannot do both. The scribe should be adept at navigating PeopleSoft Financials and should be a speedy, accurate typist to allow the meetings to keep moving. With care, these meetings will be the vehicle whereby the team is catapulted into being experts on PeopleSoft Financials and how it fits into the organization. Prototyping, or product review sessions, are an effective and efficient way to set the foundation of the software and its implementation.

Keys to successful prototyping include the following.

• Establish an appropriately furnished "command central" location.

- Ensure that the sessions are focused, regular, full-day sessions free of interruptions.
- Make sure that the decisionmaker is present at the meetings.
- The project leader should *lead* the meetings, not monopolize them.
- Provide a separate "scribe" individual responsible for operating the equipment and documenting decisions.
- Don't try to prototype too many modules at one time. The implementation team needs success and tangible benefit to keep executive management support. Focus first on key manageable modules.

The prototyping process includes the following steps.

1 Model the current business processes.
2 Identify and apply an appropriate, effective chart field configuration.
3 Discuss all installation parameters and their implications.
4 Review all business processes, panels, and fields in detail.
5 Document customization requirements.
6 Develop security access profiles.
7 Document all decisions.

chapter 8

Putting the prototype into action

One of the main outputs of the prototyping process will be detailed specifications of all customization requirements. While the end users are
implementing their business process improvements and communicating
policy changes to the organization, the programmers will take the specifications and turn them into product modifications applied to PeopleSoft
Financials. Some may wonder why an organization would purchase a
software package only to modify it. In theory, it should install the software in its base form. That would be the easiest way to have a new
system up and running. In practice, however, each industry—even each
company within an industry—has unique requirements, which the
software has to support. One of the main advantages of PeopleSoft
Financials over its competitors is its inherent extensibility. The application modules provide a framework to support the underlying business
processes. Add to that framework the ability to configure the software's
hundreds of setup parameters and the application can closely match the
requirements of each individual organization. This is never quite

enough, however. At literally every location, PeopleSoft Financials will need some level of modification before it will be functional. The key for effective customization is to understand when and how to apply these modifications and the implications they will have for the future.

8.1 The PeopleSoft upgrade architecture

A common misperception new PeopleSoft customers have is that installing a new software release is easy. PeopleSoft vociferously touts its software as innately easy to upgrade. Implementation teams can take that sound bite and quickly build a host of assumptions around it. It is common for the misinformed to claim that PeopleSoft upgrades itself: "You just run a program and it will update everything automatically." That is not remotely true, and PeopleSoft does not claim that it is. PeopleSoft does provide a mechanism for identifying and applying certain types of modifications. The software also inherently keeps track of customizations. That is a far cry from an automatic upgrade, but it is better than most software packages on the market today. To understand the impact that modifications will have for future releases, we must examine the PeopleSoft upgrade procedures.

The concept of upgrading the software to a new release is really quite simple at its root. The upgrade process requires that we compare the production version of the application with the base application of the same release and also with the base application of the new release. (See Figure 8.1.)

In traditional mainframe-based software, the upgrade process is very tedious. That is because so much of the software's functionality is buried inside of COBOL or PL1 programs. To compare one release with the next, as shown in Figure 8.1, is not practical. Vendors must document where and how new versions differ from previous ones. To skip an upgrade only means getting further behind. Even with newer software, built using fourth-generation tools, applying upgrades is still quite complex.

PeopleTools has built-in software version-tracking capabilities. Whenever a developer makes a change to a PeopleTools object, such as a record definition or a panel, when he or she saves the object, PeopleTools

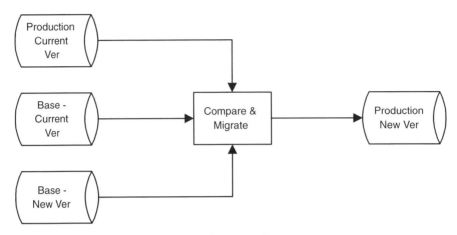

Figure 8.1 Conceptual model of application upgrade process

automatically updates the version number of the object using the current version number found in a special table, PSVER. To illustrate, let's pretend we have a new version of the General Ledger module and that it is installed with no customizations. The VERSIONNO field in the PSVER table might ship with a value of, say, 35678. That means that all objects (records, panels, menus, etc.) in the application will have VERSIONNO values of less than 35678. Furthermore, the VERSIONNO of the last object saved will be 35768. Now, suppose a developer adds a new PeopleCode program to the LEDGER record definition. Both the new PeopleCode program and the LEDGER table, when saved, will have their VERSIONNO value updated. One will be 35769 and the other will be 35770. This version-tracking procedure is the key to PeopleSoft's upgrade architecture.

When developers install the new release of the base application, its PeopleTools objects have their own VERSIONNO values. PeopleTools Application Upgrader has a compare utility, which compares version numbers for all of the objects in the new release with those of the current release. The compare process will encounter the scenarios shown in Table 8.1. There are others, but not all potential combinations are likely.

The actual compare process is a PeopleSoft program. It loads some special, PeopleTools tables with literally every object and their status, as described in Table 8.1. In addition, depending upon how the upgrade compare program is run, it will set a default action code. So, for example, it might set the default action to *Replace* the current version's, object

Table 8.1 Object status scenarios when comparing releases

Source (New)	Target (Current)	Explanation
UnChanged	UnChanged	Neither the current version nor the new version has a modification for that particular PeopleTools object.
UnChanged	Changed	Only the current version's object was modified. This would occur if a developer customized that object, but PeopleSoft did not modify it for the new release. For this situation, when applying a new release, the developer should probably opt to keep its already customized version.
UnChanged	Deleted	This would happen if a developer deleted a PeopleTools object that was left unchanged in the new release.
Changed	UnChanged	PeopleSoft modified the object as part of the new release, and in the current release it was not modified.
Changed	Changed	In this situation, the object has been modified in both databases. This requires some investigation and a decision to determine which version to apply as part of the upgrade.
Changed	Deleted	The object has been deleted in the current version, but PeopleSoft's new release contains an update to it.
Deleted	UnChanged	PeopleSoft deleted the object in the new release, and it was left unmodified in the current version. Typically, this object is no longer needed and will be deleted as part of the upgrade process.
Deleted	Changed	In this case, the current release has a modified version of the object, implying that the organization is using it for some purpose other than PeopleSoft's original intent, since the new version no longer includes it.

with the new version's when both have been Changed. So, in a nutshell, the compare process identifies all changes to the PeopleSoft application between versions, irrespective of whether they were made by PeopleSoft to the new release or by the customer to the current release. PeopleSoft also provides detailed comparison reports, so those doing the upgrade can methodically evaluate each object one by one. On the surface this may seem like a great help to the upgrade process, and rightly so. However, the real time-consuming portion of the upgrade is still manual. The upgrade team has to revisit each customization made to the current release, examining the change and understanding the business justification for it, before it can select which version of the object to keep during the upgrade. The Application Upgrader also contains a *Copy* function, which is used to actually apply the merged changes after the upgrade team has identified the appropriate action for each object.

Now assume that due to a business requirement, the implementation team customizes the Department panel and the Journal Entry panel, as well as two record definitions, eight fields, and one menu. That is a total of 13 objects changed by a single customization requirement. Fifteen months later, when the organization applies its first upgrade, those completing it will wonder why those 13 objects were changed and may indeed have no way to actually tie them together as part of the same change. The larger the degree of customization, the worse this problem becomes. It may be easy to identify which PeopleTools objects have changed, but to merge a new version with customizations release after release is difficult and time-consuming.

Hopefully, it is now clear that the upgrade architecture of PeopleSoft provides an effective means to identify where to look when applying a new software release, but the most difficult part of the process remains. Now, to provide a better context, the reader must realize that we've only been discussing changes to the *PeopleTools objects*—that is, record definitions, panels, fields, menus, trees, queries, and so forth. We've not even discussed the data tables which might have changed. Perhaps the new release has added a new field to the STATE_NAMES table. The record definition for that table will appear on our upgrade comparision, but we will still have to unload the table, alter it, and reload the data. And besides that, we've not even mentioned the batch programs. Any changes made to the standard SQR programs or the COBOL programs will have to be analyzed against the new release, and the two versions will have to be manually merged into a new release.

The bottom line about the upgrade process is that it is decidedly a manual procedure. Every customization that the implementation team makes must be revisited at each upgrade. Those modifications with large scopes might take extraordinary effort to duplicate in a new release, depending on the degree of difference between the two releases. There are some organizations that will not accept any customization requests if the impact on the upgrade will be more than minimal. So highly do they value the timely installation of new releases, that they refuse to allow noncritical functionality to impede the process. The most surprising thing about this is that it is probably the end users who are curtailing the customizations—not the development staff. It is a great example of who should be responsible for the PeopleSoft Financials, and why a proper approach to packaged application support for organizations is important.

8.2 Politics and customizations

The implementation team might meet resistance to a logical approach to software customization. As we've said, PeopleSoft Financials is marketed as nirvana for end users, because it can be so easily made to fit their requirements. Some of the end users may even attend training courses for PeopleTools and other technical topics. In organizations with central Information Systems departments, the question about who owns the application and who is responsible for customizing it can be a heated one. Precisely who will make the customizations must be determined by each organization, but PeopleSoft is not a license for them to assign amateur programmers to make changes to the system. The complexity of the software and the implications changes will have for future releases makes it dangerous to ask novice or untrained programmers to customize it.

It has been said that good programmers with bad tools will develop good systems. Bad programmers with good tools will develop poor systems. Good programmers with good tools will develop good systems faster. PeopleTools is an excellent toolset. It affords a rapid application development environment. Developers can code their programs with unprecedented speed. However, that does not negate the need for appropriate analysis

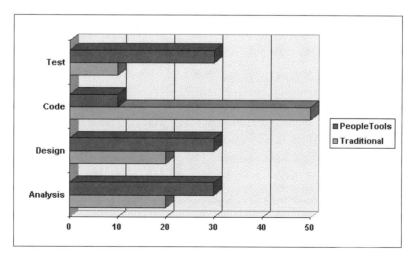

Figure 8.2 Comparison of traditional development stages versus PeopleTools development stages

and design work, as well as thorough and accurate testing. Truthfully, the greatest benefit PeopleTools offers the developers is to shorten the coding portion of the development cycle, freeing them to spend additional time in other areas to improve software quality. (See Figure 8.2.)

Whether the programmers actually sit in central Information Systems or in the end user departments is immaterial, as long as good corporate development standards and processes are followed. The implementation team must clearly communicate precisely how PeopleTools is advantageous and stress that skilled developers still must be tasked with the customizations. With any luck, the project leader will have made the case when the implementation team was created, and it will consist of these skilled developers.

8.3 Customization "best practices"

The mechanics of actually making the changes to the software are best saved for user training sessions and for reference manuals. We will focus, instead, on the keys to effective customizations. By *effective* we mean that the appropriate requirements are fulfilled efficiently and in a manner that can be supported in the long run. These "best practice" guidelines should be adopted, and the organization should see to it that the staff follows them.

8.3.1 Don't customize

The first and most important rule to remember when confronted with a change request for the software is: Don't do it! The more that PeopleSoft Financials is left as is, the easier and less expensive it will be to support. The 1994 Standish Group conducted a study about development projects and found that nearly 75 percent of all "requirements" put forth by end users were actually "blue sky" requests. It seems that end users feel as though they get only one shot at programming resources, so they are obliged to ask for everything they could possibly want. First, justify that the business requirement does truly exist and that it has the backing of the appropriate management. Then, exhaust other alternatives, such as changing the business procedures in the end user department. If that is not possible and the modification is required, only then should the organization submit a modification request.

8.3.2 Keep the upgrade in mind

If a modification to the software is unavoidable, then put it in terms of cost/benefit and be sure to gain the approval of management to complete it. The developers should communicate the expense of the customization in terms of time, money, and effort. They should also clearly state the recurring costs associated with applying the changes each time they apply a new release. Sometimes that alone will reverse the decision. At other times the costs will clearly be justified by the benefit realized by the new functionality.

It is also important for the developers to understand how the upgrade process works. At one installation, a zealous database administrator did not understand how the PeopleTools version numbers related to the upgrade process and was using database utilities to copy record definitions and panels. At upgrade time, with the version numbers meaningless, the upgrade compare procedure did not work as PeopleSoft intended. Further, understanding that every time developers save PeopleTools objects it will create another entry in the Application Upgrader compare process is critical to designing customizations that have as small an impact to the upgrade process as is possible.

8.3.3 Extend instead of modify

Another key to an effective customization strategy is to isolate the changes as much as possible. Developers can think of this as extending the software rather than changing it—for example, suppose that an organization has very strict general ledger journal entry edits and that most of them are not supported in the PeopleSoft GLEDIT COBOL program. Two ways to go about adding the edits are as follows.

1 Modify the COBOL program coding the additional edits.
2 Create a new program, probably with SQR, to perform the additional edits and insert it in the appropriate position in the GLEDIT job stream.

Of the two, the second does a far better job of isolating the changes. When PeopleSoft sends a new version of the GLEDIT COBOL program, it can simply replace the old one. The SQR program may need to be modified, but it is a self-contained program, which is well understood by the developers. The same strategy can be applied to online panel modifications. It is easier at upgrade time to have new fields in a panel group all on a single, new panel. This is not always efficient for the panel users, however, and the developers will have to find an acceptable middle ground.

8.3.4 Customize the PeopleSoft COBOL only as a last resort

PeopleSoft develops its major process-supporting offline programs using COBOL. It is well written, employing all the traditional structure-coding rules. Editing journal entries, posting payables vouchers, selecting vendor invoices for payment, and other logic-intensive programs are written in COBOL. In general, the offline processes that PeopleSoft anticipates users will want to modify are written in SQR. Other, critical processes, which users should not change, are written in COBOL.

The "Catch-22" blocking the modification of the COBOL programs is its excellent design. The COBOL programs consist of dozens and dozens of modules, which are called by other programs in a complicated nesting of modules. It is an excellent technique for isolating functions, but without detailed knowledge of their relationships, developers will have a tough time following the logic flow. PeopleSoft sends little documentation about the COBOL programs. Another complexity is that all SQL statements executed against the application database are stored in special tables in the database. It is not intuitively obvious precisely where certain logic is processed in the programs to begin with, and this strategy further clouds the issue. For these reasons, modifying the COBOL programs should be the last resort. A better strategy is to write an SQR program to manipulate the database either prior to or after the particular COBOL program runs.

8.3.5 Don't rename PeopleSoft variables

Renaming PeopleSoft variables is a cardinal sin. There is literally no excuse to ever do this. Overzealous programmers may not like it that the Product field is used to represent Machine Number, but the implications of changing the name of a field are simply too significant. The developer will have to scan every PeopleCode program and update all references to the variable. The organization will pay a major price at upgrade time to satisfy a coding zealot's search for "technical purity."

8.3.6 Hide fields, don't delete them

Another common mistake for novice PeopleSoft programmers is to remove unnecessary fields from panels to make room for new fields or to reduce the number of tabs to navigate all fields on a panel. This also will increase the number of exceptions on the upgrade reports. A better way to accomplish the same goal is to hide the fields. Users do not have to tab through hidden fields, and, though they might appear on the upgrade compare report, it will be obvious that the field was simply hidden and not removed for some unknown reason.

8.3.7 Document all modifications

We discussed previously how the most difficult aspect of applying upgrades to PeopleSoft is revisiting the reasons why a particular change was made and what all the programs and PeopleTools objects included in it were. The problem is made worse by time and by staff turnover. The implementation team should establish a mechanism to guarantee that all changes to the software are carefully and thoroughly documented. Developers should record the following information about each change they make to the software.

- Who requested the change
- The developer who completed the change
- The end user contact (functional expert)
- When the change was made
- Why the change was made (business justification)
- How the change was made (technical description)
- All PeopleTools objects and programs that were changed as part of the customization
- Screen-print of any panel changes involved

Many organizations have found that an effective way to track software customizations is to build a system, using PeopleTools, right in the financial database. By defining several records, panels, and reports that

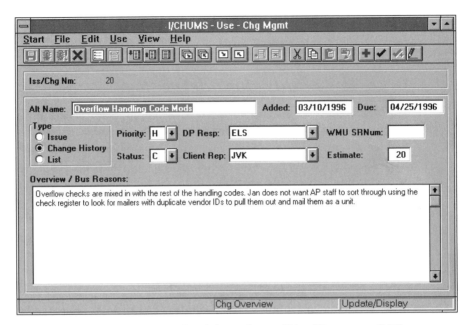

Figure 8.3 Panel 1 contains overview information and identifies responsibilities

can track this information, developers can document the changes and the reasons for them right in with the application. If an organization decides to change hardware or database platforms, these application notes are simply migrated with the rest of the PeopleSoft applications. It is also beneficial because the documentation platform is the same as the programming one, which makes it natural for developers to document as they program. (See Figure 8.3.)

This integrated, changed management system can be as simple or complex as the implementation team feels is necessary. Some PeopleSoft customers have built entire project management repositories to identify and track project tasks and schedules and produce status reports. That may be necessary for sites planning major customizations, but for most installations, a simple means to store the how and why of each customization is critical if the upgrade process is to be fast and efficient. (See Figure 8.4.)

Keys to effective customization include the following.

- Understand the PeopleSoft upgrade process.

- Assign programming assignments to qualified developers.

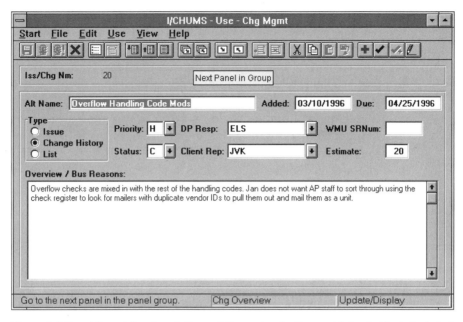

Figure 8.4 Panel 2 contains descriptions of the customization and lists of objects included

- Customizing should be the last resort.
- Keep the upgrade process in mind when designing modifications.
- Extend instead of modify.
- Don't modify the COBOL programs.
- Don't rename variables.
- Hide fields, don't delete them from panels.
- Document, document, document all customizations.

8.4 Business process improvement

Another output of the prototype sessions is the list of changes to the organization's business processes, operational requirements, and policies. These might range from drastic to minor. Whatever the scope, the end users, while the programmers are applying the customizations, must set about putting the changes in motion. Each organization will have its own political system, and the team must pay heed to it. However, People-Soft can be the beginning of the end of major politics if executive management strongly supports these process changes. Change, itself, elicits different responses from different personality types. Organizations consist of various personality types, and some people will welcome the improvements, while others will be afraid of them or even aggressively oppose them. Understanding this from the beginning is important, so the implementation team does not lose heart when the latter group fires the first shots of criticism. There are a few strategies that can help turn these changes into a positive for the team.

8.4.1 Tell everyone everything—set expectations

Hide nothing. That is a cardinal rule of the new, information-based organization. Knowledge is traditionally power. Sharing the decisions, the business rules, the justifications, and the benefits with everyone levels the playing field. There are no winners and no losers, only sound business decisions. Failure to set the expectations leads to surprised individuals, who will react emotionally. Expectations are critical to success. At its root, success is a subjective judgment on the part of someone who has authority to reward or punish. By setting the expectations and then following through with them, the team will build credibility and trust. When a hungry person goes into a fast-food restaurant to buy some food, the expectations are that the food will curb his or her hunger, but won't really be very good. When the clerk delivers the cheeseburger and fries, the customer is satisfied, because this is what was expected. On the other hand, if that same person orders a cheeseburger and fries from a five-star restaurant, and the waiter hands this person a fast-food "value meal," he or she will be livid, because more was expected. Set the expectations by being brutally honest.

8.4.2 Ask for input, if possible

People always want to be part of the process. They may not want to invest any time or effort, but they want their voice heard. As much as possible, the implementation team should seek the advice of key personnel affected by the changes. Even if their ideas are not feasible, simply listening can send the message that the PeopleSoft project stands for quality improvement and not politics as usual.

8.4.3 Market the benefits

The changes to the business processes will come with some tangible benefits, or the team would not be implementing them. Even if changes are justified by bottom-line cost savings, there will be benefits. The team must consistently and continuously trumpet these benefits. Changes that benefit other parts of the organization are the most important ones to tout. Politicians know that if they say something often enough and loud enough, even if it is blatantly false, it is eventually perceived as the truth. The implementation team must learn this lesson and champion the PeopleSoft project and the improvements it will bring.

8.4.4 Secure executive support

It should be easy to gain the backing of the executive management. If the implementation is progressing as planned, management will be compelled to endorse these organizational changes to support their investment in PeopleSoft Financials. Since every organization has "show-me" individuals, who will not get behind anything new until it has proven itself, executive support can guarantee that these people at least abide by the changes. They will eventually come around, but until then, they can simply be told, "Do it."

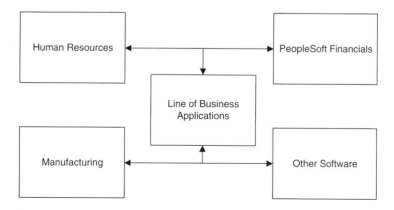

Figure 8.5 Interfaces with other software

The specifics involved in these process changes vary significantly from organization to organization, and it is impractical to delve into the details of specific processes here. Process improvement is a major ingredient to a successful implementation, however, and the project team has to effectively bring it about. Without it, PeopleSoft will be less than optimal. Presumably, the organization purchased PeopleSoft Financials in support of the basic corporate premise: the profit motive. If it does not help to improve the performance of the organization, then it is probably a waste of money. Process improvement and policy changes are a big part of that and are critical to the project's success.

8.5 *Building interfaces*

Whenever an organization buys a packaged software application from a vendor, it must build bridges from it to its other software systems. This is also true with PeopleSoft Financials. Fortunately, PeopleSoft provides interfaces between its own product modules. Purchasing sends information into Accounts Payable, which sends information to General Ledger, and so on. However, most organizations have additional software systems, which must communicate if the organization is to operate effectively. (See Figure 8.5.)

Designing and building the interfaces will be mostly a programming task. It will not require significant input from end users and other implementation team members. Programmers can begin coding the interfaces almost as soon as the team completes the chart field customization. Where there are areas of uncertainty, the programmers can seek the advice of the implementation team by attending a prototype session to ask questions and solidify specifications. In many cases, PeopleSoft provides a vehicle to load data to its database. General Ledger includes a journal-loading SQR program, which programmers can either modify for its installation or write a program to precede the PeopleSoft program. In Purchasing, PeopleSoft provides a program to batch load requisitions.

These are excellent starting points for interfaces *to* PeopleSoft Financials, but what about interfaces *from* PeopleSoft Financials? Unfortunately, they are puzzles for the programmers to solve. To complete these interfaces, the programmers will need to understand the design of the PeopleSoft database. The software has thousands of fields in dozens of tables. Add to that the complexity of effective dating and history, current and future data rows, and the task of culling data from PeopleSoft Financials to import into other applications. Interfaces are excellent candidates for the assistance of a PeopleSoft implementation partner. It will take some time for the organization to develop its knowledge of the database. Assigning a knowledgeable consultant familiar with PeopleSoft and an in-house programmer who knows the other applications is an effective way to ensure acceptable progress on the interfaces.

Whatever the strategy, the programmers must design and build the interfaces with portability in mind. The safest strategy is to build each interface using two programs: One should be an SQR program to extract data from other systems, and the other should be a program using the most appropriate language to import the data into the new system. This isolates the two applications from one another and also isolates the changes needed, in the event that one of the systems is eventually modified or replaced. (See Figure 8.6.)

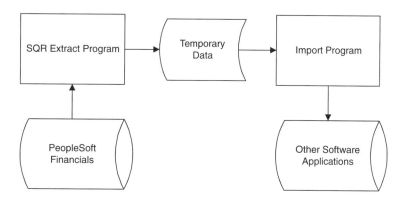

Figure 8.6 Interface design to isolate applications from one another

Besides adopting a good design, the programmers must also carefully document the interfaces. It will take a great deal of research to define the interfaces and to build and test them. It is ludicrous to squander this knowledge by letting it fade from the memories of those who have it. The implementation team should require the programmers to document the interface specifications in great detail. Interfaces are not processes that are often modified. Four years later, when the interface requirements change, a new programmer can take the interface documentation and quickly get up to speed. It is a classic "pay me now or pay me later" issue, and this is an opportunity the team should take advantage of.

Designing and building interface keys should include the following steps.

1   Start with the PeopleSoft interface programs.

2   Use an implementation partner, if possible.

3   Design interfaces for portability.

4   Document the interface requirements in detail.

8.6 *Financial reporting*

The financial reporting environment will evolve naturally once PeopleSoft is fully implemented. However, organizations do have both internal and external reporting requirements, which must be met. Typically, operational reports are used to support the daily business operations. Many of these reports will have new counterparts in PeopleSoft Financials. Some, however, will not. The implementation team must determine which reports are truly required for the software to move to production. That should be the entire focus. It must not include the wider scope of information access or organization-wide access to reports and queries, unless the project team has the resources to include these in the implementation. Presumably, during the prototyping sessions, the implementation team analyzed these requirements. The reports that were identified as essential must be created and tested in preparation for the move to production.

chapter 9

Production

We have been discussing the various issues associated with the implementation of PeopleSoft Financials, but the ultimate goal is to get the software into production. The project team can spend months and months preparing for the event, but it will eventually have to put the preparation into production. Putting a major information systems project into production is akin to giving birth. Months of gestation and anticipation culminate in an excruciating delivery. The stretch of time it takes to switch to the new software is not excessively lengthy, but it is an intense one. It is a whirlwind of last-minute changes, bug fixes, problem resolutions, and the like. After a time, the tide of problems ebbs to a manageable level, and the software simply idles along appropriately, only requiring minor attention to keep running. Before it can make the transition to production, however, the implementation team must complete some additional tasks.

9.1 Data conversion

The data conversion effort can range from extremely minor to enormous. Defined, data conversion is really the mapping of data fields from one set of database files into data fields of another set of database files. The more complex the source database, the more difficult the conversion will be. PeopleSoft provides several tools to facilitate data conversion. Mapping the data, however, is a decidedly manual process. In addition, it can be another politically sensitive issue. Data ownership and data access are not always clearly defined. Different individuals or departments may define certain terms differently. To properly accomplish the conversion, the implementation team will need to bring these people to consensus.

The first step of data conversion is to determine its scope. It is important to ensure that the data conversion phases closely match the phases of the project itself. If the first phase is general ledger *only,* then the data conversion programmers should spend little time analyzing the purchasing data. How much of the data to convert also must be determined. Most sites will want to load some level of historical information. Precisely how much history and of which kind will have organization-wide impact. The implementation team must decide on and communicate the level of and types of data that will be converted, to avoid surprises down the road.

The next step of data conversion is data mapping—identifying fields in the old source database and locating their target and format in People-Soft Financials. Some of the elements will be easy, but others will not. The data mappers will need to establish some methods and accounting mechanisms to ensure that each and every data element from the old system is appropriately carried to the PeopleSoft database. From another viewpoint, they will have to ensure that all fields required in PeopleSoft Financials are correctly entered. These are actually two separate requirements, because the old system and the new system will not have a one-to-one match of fields. More than likely, the old database will be much smaller than PeopleSoft, with far fewer data elements. In many old, in-house financial systems, the team may be mapping data from ten or 20 files to over 150 relational tables. (See Figure 9.1.)

An excellent place to start is to study the PeopleSoft data models. They are included with the system's documentation, and they provide an overview of what types of data are in the system. Relational databases are designed using data-entity concepts. It is helpful if the data mappers

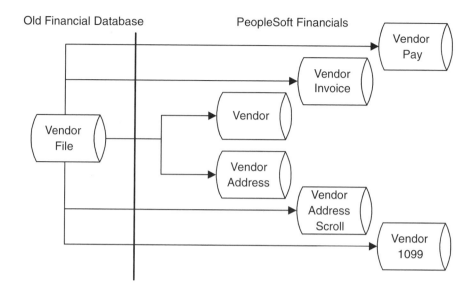

Figure 9.1 Sample mapping of a single vendor file to six database tables in PeopleSoft

understand the concepts of relational database design, at least at a basic level, so they'll have a context in which to place the data models. Presumably, knowledge of the old system will be available to the implementation team. Once the data mappers have a solid comprehension of both databases, they can begin to define how to convert the data. Some will create a formal, detailed, and meticulous set of procedures and controls, while others will simply "hack" together conversion programs. Whatever the methods, the team must meet two requirements. First, the data conversion cannot go on indefinitely. Structured coding and software engineering principles must take a back seat to raw productivity. Do not allow technical purists to slow down the data conversion. These programs, ideally, will run only once. They are not worth any effort that will ultimately slow down the process. The second requirement is to provide a mechanism both to track whether or not all of the required data fields are converted and to communicate the logic of the data mapping to the end users.

Going hand in hand with the need to promptly complete the data conversion is the issue of *how much* of the data to actually convert. Literally no data conversion undertaking can copy 100 percent of the data, error free, to PeopleSoft Financials. The implementation team must make that clear from the outset. Each data conversion will have a point at which further efforts are counterproductive. At that instant, data must simply be converted. Errors and exceptions can be cleaned up, online, in the new system by the end users. Some may balk at this, but, with appropriate forewarning, at least they will not be surprised. To visualize this, let's take the conversion of vendors into PeopleSoft format. The VENDOR table consists of a number of fields containing identifying information about vendors. Vendor ID, name, status, and other information are housed in the VENDOR table. One specific field that is used to access and look up vendors is the VENDOR_SHORTNAME. It is a ten-position field, which is a sort of "nickname" for a vendor. That way, rather than entering "Coca-Cola Bottling Company of Michigan" to select a vendor or remembering a meaningless, ten-character VENDOR_ID, the users simply enter the VENDOR_SHORTNAME. In our example, it might be "COCA" or "COKE." To further complicate things, it is a unique field. Assuming our old vendor file only has a vendor number and a name, how do we go about creating the VENDOR_SHORTNAME field? If we simply take the first ten positions of the description, we get "COCA-COLA" which is not what we want. This is an example of a field where the conversion effort can establish a base, which the end users will need to manually audit and update.

The data conversion programmers should function as a SWAT team. They should get in, get the job done effectively and efficiently, and then get out. The organization must not allow the end user departments to insist on a perfect data conversion. Data conversion is good enough when it is complete enough to support PeopleSoft Financials in production. Anything further is probably overkill. There are occasions, too, when it is more cost-effective to hire temporary keypunch operators to enter data rather than undergo the rigors of a data conversion. This is unusual, but it illustrates the point that the focus of the conversion should be to facilitate getting PeopleSoft in production.

9.2 Conversion tools

The logistics of how to copy data from an old financial application into a PeopleSoft application are unique to each organization. The old software and its accompanying database will differ drastically from installation to installation. One organization might have an IMS database; another a

COBOL, VSAM combination; and others might be scaling upwards from a PC-based financial application. Because of this, conversion programs are often two-step processes. The first step is to extract the data from the old database. The second is to import the data into the PeopleSoft database. Buried somewhere within those two steps will be data manipulation logic to transform fields and values in the old system to fields and values in the new one. Quite often, each step will be its own program and, because of PeopleSoft's conversion tools, that is frequently the most efficient configuration. (See Figure 9.2.)

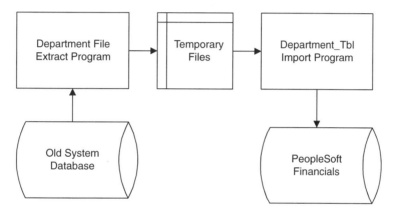

Figure 9.2 Example of a typical conversion process

9.2.1 Data extracting tools

There is little to say about tools required to extract data from the old application database. Each organization will have its own. Some might use COBOL or PL1, while others will use SAS or C++. More than likely, the data conversion programmers will have existing tools and utilities to help them write data extract programs, and it is a great opportunity for legacy programmers with knowledge of the old system to get involved with the PeopleSoft project. These programs will probably have a significant amount of logic in them to massage and transform the data from the old format into the new one. The programs will output temporary files, which will be used as input to the import tools.

9.2.2 Import Manager

The simplest tool for moving data into PeopleSoft is the Import Manager (see Figure 9.3). Import Manager is a PeopleTools tool that reads data from a flat file and inserts it into the appropriate table in PeopleSoft. Using the Import Manager is relatively easy. It includes the following steps.

1   Select a table from the database to be the import target.

2   Identify the location of the sequential source file.

3   Specify the starting location, length, and format, in the source file, of each field.

4   Specify value conversions for appropriate fields—for example, a "B" in the source field might translate to "PAY" in the target PeopleSoft table.

5   Run the import in Edit mode and examine the errors and exceptions report.

6   Fix any errors, either by adjusting the import definition or adjusting the old system extract program, to create a new import sequential file.

7   Run the import in Load mode and verify the errors and exceptions report.

Steps 4–6 will be iterative until the import is deemed clean enough to run the final load. The error reports will be important because many of the potential import errors are obscure. That is because the Import Manager executes certain types of PeopleCode programs against each record as it is imported. These types of programs include the following.

- FieldEdit
- FieldFormula
- RowInit
- SaveEdit
- SavePostChg
- SavePreChg

Imports can face performance problems, because they run on the client and because PeopleTools executes the PeopleCode programs for each row. It may take as long as eight hours to import a single large table,

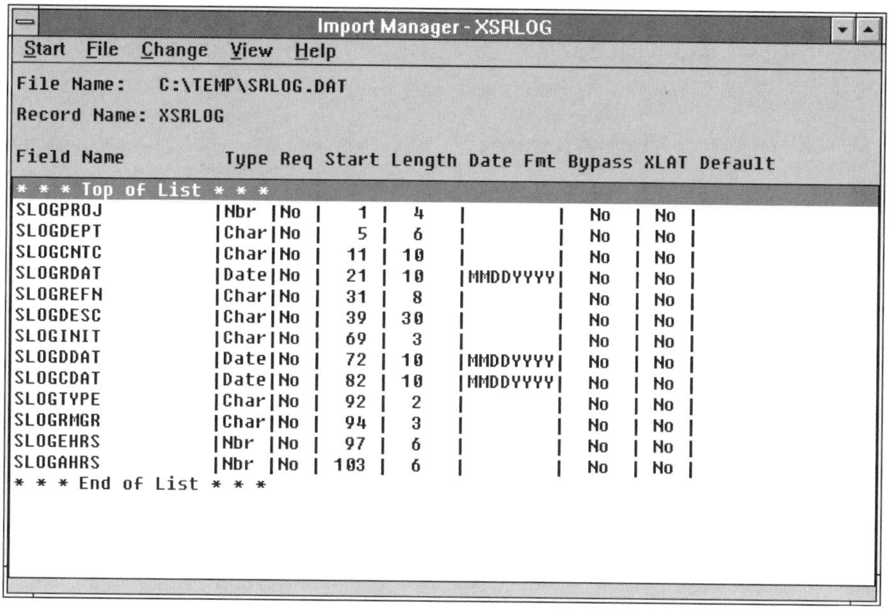

Figure 9.3 Import Manager

which may be unacceptable. One strategy to circumvent this performance bottleneck is to split the source file into several files and run the import simultaneously from multiple machines. In our eight-hour example, if we split the import file into four files and run the import from four machines at the same time, it should finish in two or three hours. It is important to test the performance of various imports before developing the final conversion plan. Import times vary drastically from table to table, and the project timeline must anticipate these times accurately.

9.2.3 SQR

Another tool that the data conversion programmers can use to load data to the PeopleSoft database is SQR. Using SQR, they can read a sequential file one row at a time, perform complex logic and calculations on it, and insert it into the target database. The benefits of SQR include the ability to perform complex procedural logic and the ability to fully access the relational database by using SQL and Data Manipulation Language (Update, Insert, Delete) statements. SQR is prevalent in the PeopleSoft offline programming, so this is a good time to acquaint the implementation team with it.

9.2.4 Data Mover

Data Mover is PeopleSoft's platform-independent data management tool. Programmers can create Data Mover scripts to load and unload data. The advantages of Data Mover over the Import Utility are performance and flexibility. The disadvantage is that Data Mover does not execute the PeopleCode edits against the data.

More than likely, the data conversion team will utilize a combination of these and other programming tools to complete the conversion effort. It will be difficult, and it must be kept on schedule. The implementation team must identify and estimate all conversion tasks in order to accurately predict a "go live" date. Despite its complexity, it is an excellent opportunity to employ legacy programmers. It affords them the chance to gain experience with relational database technology and the new programming tools. With proper care, the conversion will not slow the progress of the PeopleSoft implementation, and it will be the springboard from which the move to production begins.

Keys to successful data conversion include the following.

- Determine the scope of the data conversion first.
- Map the data from the old system to the new methodically to ensure all appropriate fields are included.
- Study and know the PeopleSoft data models.
- Realize that for conversion programs, coding efficiency is more important than engineering principles.
- Use the 90%/10% rule to determine the completeness of the conversion programs.
- Use a combination of best-fit tools to maximize programmer productivity.
- Include legacy programmers with knowledge of source databases.

9.3 *Testing*

Of all the steps involved in building or installing software, besides documentation, testing is the one that developers most often neglect. It is not that they do not believe in testing, because they do. It is more a function of "developer arrogance"—that is, "I built the software, I know what it does, and I know it works." In fact, developers are terrible testers, because they see the software through their own paradigm rather than through that of an end users. A careful programmer might test a program for hours, only to have an end user "break" it within five minutes by doing something that the programmer never foresaw. For this reason, there are multiple types of testing that must be accomplished before the cutover to production.

9.3.1 *Software acceptance testing*

The base starting point for the implementation should be a working "vanilla" system. That means that the software should function as expected, including all the offline processes the organization plans to use. Most generally, acceptance testing is included as a part of the software installation. By ensuring that all the processes work correctly and that offline programs complete appropriately, the developers can be reasonably sure that if something does not work, it is a result of a change made by them rather than a bug in the base software. Some may wonder why a vendor package would need to be tested upon installation. The answer is quite simple. No vendor can anticipate all possible configurations its customers will use. A group of unattached settings does carry the potential to introduce a bug into the software. By performing a detailed test on the software before it is customized, the implementation team can begin building on a stable, known software system.

9.3.2 *Unit testing*

Each programmer who modifies portions of PeopleSoft Financials should be held responsible for verifying that these portions function, in isolation, according to specifications. Unit testing is most often the programmer's responsibility. In the best of circumstances, another developer performs unit testing, but most likely not. Unit testing involves running the program code and processes through various potential scenarios and seeing that the ouputs agree with expected results. If a programmer were tasked to see that only the accounting department has authority to deactivate a Department_ID on the Department_Tbl chart field, it is his or her responsibility to make the change and then test it with the various security profiles to verify that it works correctly. Typically, developers perform unit testing as a part of their job. The project leader simply needs to remind them to do so.

9.3.3 Integration testing

Software developers are less likely to perform adequate integration testing. Integration testing, as its name suggests, tests the reliability and accuracy of the software as a whole. Unit testing has already verified that the individual pieces function properly, but with multiple programmers working on the same project, ensuring that the individual components work correctly once they are assembled is critical. In software, minor inconsistencies between components, when propogated throughout the entire system, can become major software bugs. Integration testing uncovers these situations, so the developers can work together and resolve them.

To be adequate, integration testing should take into account two specific types of testing. The first is to carefully and precisely test circumstances that are known to exist, especially those that required customizations to accommodate them. If the accounts payable department receives invoices that contain multiple line items, some of which are applicable to Federal 1099 reporting and others that are not, then the integration testing should include this test scenario. It is impossible to test for every combination of circumstances in integration test, so the team should focus on those which are either most common, most critical or for which they have customized the software.

The second type of testing is "typical-day" testing. A typical day's work will contain a variety of random circumstances and a more appropriate volume. By entering a day's work into the PeopleSoft application, the end users can evaluate the actual results and see how closely they match expected results for a given day. It also provides a sample to estimate elapsed time for various procedures and program runs. The integration testing process needs to include all processes that will run once the new system is in production. Data entry, edits, audits, posting, and interfaces should all be included. When specific test cases are combined with a typical day's work, it provides a solid foundation for verifying the accuracy of PeopleSoft Financials as a software *system*.

9.3.4 Stress testing

Another oft-neglected phase of testing is stress testing. Presumably, the hardware and operating system platform of the database server has been carefully selected to provide adequate horsepower to support PeopleSoft Financials. However, the implementation team will not be able to reliably predict the performance of such a complex client/server software application. Stress testing involves running the application at peak volume levels to ascertain whether it will stand up against a heavy processing day. Nothing can ruin the reputation of a software application more than its inability to provide high enough performance levels for end users to complete their work.

The online portion of PeopleSoft Financials should be tested with a full load of users pounding away entering transactions. If completed appropriately, the stress testing can coincide with the "day's work" portion of the integration testing. It will require that entire end user departments spend concentrated time together, entering data into the system and running processes and reports. That can be difficult, because they will have their regular work to complete, too. Weekends are excellent times to do stress testing from an operational viewpoint, but they do not represent reality. Typically, the network traffic and perhaps even the database server will have much lighter loads during weekends and off-hours. To truly evaluate the performance, the online stress testing must occur when the rest of the organization is working at full force.

The offline process can and should be tested at times that are similar to the actual planned production schedule. If the general ledger journal entry edit program is designated to run at 9:00 P.M., then that is when it should run. The database server should be running its typical load for that time as well.

The implementation team should leave enough time between the stress testing and the scheduled cutover date to address and correct any performance problems revealed during this testing. When there is not enough time to do this, then the developers spend time during and after cutover just trying to tune the application to be able to keep up. A week or two should be ample time to make any minor adjustments. Unless the network, workstations, or database server are grossly incapable, this should be sufficient. If the testing reveals major performance problems and the need to replace one or more of the underlying client/server infrastructures, then the project team will have to negotiate this with end users and executive management. It is better to be honest and admit a mistake up front than to hide the problem and let it be discovered once the software is in production. In general, errors are much less expensive to fix before they occur than after they occur. Thorough stress testing will see to it that PeopleSoft Financials is ready and capable to support the organization when it is moved into production.

9.3.5 Parallel testing

Parallel testing is the process of comparing the results of the new software with those of the existing software. It is not always done officially, but is done at some level unless the organization is moving from a completely manual system to PeopleSoft Financials. In that instance, there would be no existing system against which to compare. In most circumstances, however, parallel testing is a necessary step before production. It verifies that the software can support the volume of transactions, and it verifies that its accuracy is acceptable. Parallel testing is specific to each implementation, because the degree of difference in business rules, as well as the level of automation in the old system, affects the scope and complexity of the testing, as well as the ease with which the project team can compare results. In the end, however, parallel testing must provide reasonable assurance to end users, programmers, and executive management that the new software is functioning appropriately and is production ready.

9.4 Production cutover

There is not much that can be said about the actual cutover into production. It will be an exciting time to say the least. Turmoil, firefighting, grenade launching: All of the typical characteristics of major change will manifest themselves at this time. The implementation team must prepare itself and its customers to survive the onslaught and to make a smooth transition to PeopleSoft Financials.

The actual process of moving the application into production is a tedious and relatively manual one. Presumably, all data conversion is complete, with last-minute tweaks having been applied. The customizations are finished and tested and the end users are trained and prepared for the change. The implementation team has to unplug the old system and plug in the new one within a small window of time. Basically, one day the end users use the old software, and the next day they come to work as PeopleSoft people. Between those times, the developers must make any last-minute changes, data conversions and program modifications identified during testing, deactivate old programs and processes, and replace them with PeopleSoft programs and processes. They also have to unhook the interfaces between the old system and other systems and replace them with the new ones that the team developed. In some cases this can be accomplished during the week. In others, it will take a weekend to complete all of the tasks.

The implementation team should build a cutover checklist and be sure that each step is assigned and completed. No development team ever feels completely ready to make the move, but it is important for this team to get a "win." No doubt, the eyes of scrutiny will be upon the PeopleSoft Financials project, because it represents a fundamental change in computing and information for the organization. It is a time that will have a lasting effect on the reputation of the team and its members. Success will breed confidence, and executive management may be willing to open the doors to even more beneficial and fundamental changes. Failure might mean that the project is canceled, and the team's future could be in jeopardy. In spite of the risk, if the implementation team is reasonably confident that it can support the move to production and any problems that will occur, then it should take the plunge. Due to the massive amount of change and the volume of tasks to complete, it is important for the implementation team to properly set expectations for this event.

Expectations of production cutover include the following.

- Expect between one and three weeks of problems.
- Be sure the implementation team is 100 percent dedicated and available around the clock for that period of time.
- Be sure that end users are committed to perform any extra work required to support the cutover.

- Communicate to executive management that the team is moving PeopleSoft into production and that it will take a few weeks to iron out all of the wrinkles.
- Be sure that network specialists and database adminstrators are available for support if necessary.

Starting with the first day that PeopleSoft is in production, some representative from the implementation team should be constantly available to the end user department. The beginning will be hectic, but slowly, day by day, sanity will set in and the end users will settle into a new routine. Gradually, the end users can be weaned from the constant support line. They will be able to solve their own problems and answer many of their own questions, and the support of the application software can fall to those who will have it for the long run. At that point, which should be a few weeks later, the implementation, at least that phase of it, is complete. To boost morale and recharge the batteries, the implementation team should be granted some debriefing time during which the team members can relax at work, catch up on administrative chores, and take some time off to catch up on tasks at home. This debriefing time is essential to the long-term health and productivity of the team. Short-term stress is an excellent motivator, but one needs time to recover from it. Without it, the stress becomes long-term and affects the attitudes and productivity, not to mention the physical health, of the project team.

Once they have had a chance to recuperate, the team members will be ready to go on to their next assignment. Assuming the implementation was successful, it is important that they are recognized for their efforts. The project leader should make sure that credit is given to the team as a whole. At no time should he or she take credit for the success, because that alienates the rest of the team. Implementing PeopleSoft Financials is laborious, and it takes an entire team to accomplish it. Appropriate recognition will be noticed and appreciated by the team. So, with the software in production and the project basically completed, the only tasks remaining are ongoing ones. Procedures such as upgrades, performance tuning, and financial reporting figuratively begin when the project ends. PeopleSoft upgrades are beyond the scope of this book and reporting is covered in the next chapter, but it is important to examine the performance-tuning requirements, since the issue will certainly surface shortly after the cutover.

9.5 Performance tuning

Performance tuning any client/server application is much more difficult than it is for traditional, mainframe-based applications, and PeopleSoft is no exception. In traditional software, all performance variables are contained within the run unit on a single platform. Developers can examine program execution times, the frequency that specific statements are executed, and also the efficiency of the database organization easily and within a single operating environment. Client/server architectures spread those variables out over multiple heterogenous operating environments and add additional parameters to the mix. Due to its complexity, performance tuning is a methodical and on-going process. Several steps are critical to its success and the perceptions of the application's performance in general.

9.5.1 Set proper performance expectations

PeopleSoft will not come close to matching the perceived performance of other, more traditional application software. There is no way, until workstation, network, and database performance standards increase dramatically, to duplicate subsecond response times, which are common in older, transaction-based software applications. There are several reasons for this.

- The introduction of the network into the mix will cause a slower response time. Since the client must communicate with the database over network wire, which is shared by perhaps hundreds of other users, it will not be as fast as if it were on the same machine.

- The complexity and functional capability of PeopleSoft Financials will inherently slow it down, as well. Simply put, software that has more to do will take longer to run than software that has less to do.

- Relational databases, when compared with other, traditional database engines, are relatively slow. To access data in a database, the client must send an SQL statement, which is really a small specific computer program. The database engine compiles the SQL into a set of machine instructions to access the data. Since PeopleSoft uses almost exclusively dynamic SQL, the database must compile the

SQL statements each time they are invoked, adding overhead to data access.

- PeopleSoft's implementation of panel groups is another reason for slower online performance. This needs to be clarified as *perceived* performance. In a traditional system, most often a single screen accesses a single, or at most a few, database file. In order to completely enter an accounts payable voucher, for example, end users might have to access as many as five or more screens. They perceive that each screen is saved quickly. They do not realize that they are saving five times, which makes the actual save time much greater. PeopleSoft uses panel groups organized to support a process. The end user enters the required information in a series of panels and then presses the save button only once. This process orientation is more efficient and does negate some of the performance losses.

This last reason needs to be the focal point for the implementation team. By touting the benefits of PeopleSoft and explaining that it may seem to be significantly slower, but the actual flow of work is actually more efficient, the end users can grow to accept the slower response time as a benefit. Further, PeopleSoft contains much more thorough data editing than is typically found in traditional application software. By eliminating errors before they find their way into the system, PeopleSoft frees the end users from a significant amount of rework. Rework is a major target in any process improvement effort, because it is almost always more expensive to fix mistakes than to prevent them. The implementation team must market the software as just that and own up to the fact that online response time will be slower. The end users will realize the benefits when they see fewer problems and higher quality, with massive improvements in access to timely information.

9.5.2 Record benchmark timings

A good place to begin the performance-tuning process is to record benchmark times. Using the major process employed by end users, the tuners should time their elapsed time during a "no-load" situation. In other words, with nothing else running on the server or the workstation, and with a minimal network load, they should record the time of each process. They should do this early in the cutover to production, as timings will change as the distribution of the data in the database changes.

These benchmarks can then be used as comparisons for performance-improvement efforts.

9.5.3 Determine what to tune

We know some things will need to be tuned, but how do we know what to tune? Generally speaking, the end users will make known those processes that take an excessively long time. Those with the worst performance should generally be tuned before those with better, relative performance, but frequency of use must be included in the equation. It is pointless to tune a process that is used once a month and takes three minutes to complete, when there are other processes that are used 20 times each hour and take twenty seconds each to save. So, basically, the tuners should focus on those programs and processes that hold the greatest potential improvements. Typically, these will be the ones the end users targets first.

Another spur to tune a process will occur when a process's performance negatively affects the performance of other, possibly unrelated, processes. Realize that a single, runaway SQL statement carries the potiential to consume all resources on the largest mainframe computer. A missing or incorrect index or an erroneous SQL statement might bring an organization's entire computing environment to its knees. The bottom line is: The order in which the processes and programs should be tuned will make itself known.

How to tune Tuning client/server applications is as much an art as a science. Each component of the software's platform will have its own, unique tuning processes, but there is no way to simultaneously analyze the performance of all pieces. Utilizing the following concepts, the tuners can methodically target and analyze poorly performing processes.

- Eliminate the workstation from the beginning. End users should have the fastest workstations possible. If they do, then the workstation can usually be eliminated as the culprit from the outset. A quick check of the same process from another workstation, however, will verify that the workstation is not the culprit.

- Ensure that database administrators are consistently maintaining the database management system. They must update statistics for those databases that require it, and they must also monitor table space and disk space status and adjust them when needed.

- Focus first on the program or process itself. If it is an SQR, for example, which is joining two large tables and returning only a few rows, it might be more efficient to remove the table join and to fetch each row from the second table directly. In order to analyze the processing options of the SQL statement, the developer will need access to the database utilities which explain how they access the data. For this reason, program tuning is closely linked with database tuning.

- Link the program tuning closely with database tuning. SQL is a boon for developers, but it seems as though its major goal in life is the consumption of CPU cycles. In most cases, the greatest performance gains will be found by analyzing SQL statements and how the database identifies an access path for them. Quite often, an SQL statement, especially one that results from customization, requires an additional index to perform acceptably. Each database has its own SQL analysis tools, and the database administrator will know how to use them.

- Test SQL statements before writing programs. In other words, if a developer is going to write a program or modify a panel to include an SQL statement, he or she should write and test it using several different syntax arrangements to find the one that performs the best. It has been found that even the order of the tables in the SQL FROM clause can affect performance dramatically. Each database has its own guidelines, and programmers should consult the documentation and the database administrators to find out what they are. In the following code segment, Query A might perform differently than Query B.

```
Query A                             Query B
SELECT A.DESCR,                     SELECT A.DESCR,
       B.ACCOUNT,                          B.ACCOUNT,
       B.AMOUNT                            B.AMOUNT
  FROM PS_DEPARTMENT_TBL A          FROM PS_LEDGER B
       PS_LEDGER B                       PS_DEPARTMENT_TBL A
 WHERE B.BUSINESS_UNIT = 'XYZ'      WHERE B.BUSINESS_UNIT = 'XYZ'
   AND B.LEDGER = 'ACTUALS'          AND B.LEDGER = 'ACTUALS'
   AND B.FISCAL_YEAR = '1999'        AND B.FISCAL_YEAR = '1999'
   AND B.ACCTG_PERIOD = 6            AND B.ACCTG_PERIOD = 6
   AND A.SETID = 'XYZ'              AND A.SETID = 'XYZ'
   AND A.DEPTID = B.DEPTID          AND A.DEPTID = B.DEPTID
```

- Assuming no additional network problems are evident, this is probably the last place to look. Network bottlenecks can exist, however, and often are difficult to pinpoint. By carefully examining the timings using PeopleSoft's SQL traces and using the database statistics to examine SQL run times, tuners can determine the percentage of time that the SQL statement spends at the database versus traversing the network. If the network timings are found to be excessive, then the networking specialists will have to provide solutions to resolve that issue. PeopleSoft traditionally has had network performance problems with its DB2 installations, due primarily to the poor performance of the IBM, LU6.2 network interacting with the underlying database communication protocols. They now provide another TCP/IP workstation-to-mainframe communication option, which eliminates that bottleneck for DB2 sites.

The tuning efforts are an ongoing affair with PeopleSoft Financials. Organizations must involve the right people in the tuning process, being certain it gets assigned appropriate priority. In the beginning, tuning requirements will be steady. Soon, however, the software will stabilize at acceptable performance levels. Then, developers and end users can monitor performance and tune only when problems occur. Those people delegated to tune PeopleSoft Financials can be successful, as long as the organization realizes that it is one of the fixed costs of owning and operating a client/server software application and that it takes time and consistency.

chapter 10

Financial reporting

One of the most common reasons why organizations replace their financial application software is because their existing systems fall woefully short of meeting ever-changing reporting requirements. PeopleSoft's corporate identity is built upon the premise that information must be pushed outward to an organization's farthest reaches. PeopleSoft Financials reflects that vision by providing an impressive array of reporting and information-retrieval tools.

To simply call it reporting is to miss the vision of PeopleSoft and the new corporation. The world's economy is shifting to an information-based one. Information assets outweigh capital assets in most large organizations. Workers are becoming more than machine operators or robots, who repetitively carry out mundane processes invented by their supervisors. Instead, to keep pace with the competition, they are being asked to assume more responsibility and make decisions of their own. To do this effectively, they need access to accurate and timely information. Simply put, organizations that make better decisions win their industry's competitive race. Traditional reporting was never designed with this type of decision support in mind. Its goal has always been to support the operational requirements.

PeopleSoft provides a reporting environment to meet both operational and informational needs.

Report generation with PeopleSoft Financials is at times effortless and, at other times, confusing. PeopleSoft ships a wealth of standard reports with its software systems, but they never fill organizational needs completely. End users ask several different types of reporting questions, and PeopleTools includes no fewer than five separate reporting tools. Deciding when and how to use which tool to answer specific reporting questions can be a daunting task. It is essential that developers and end users understand the types of reports and the different report-creation tools. It is also critical that organizations establish guidelines on their use. Failure to do so can lead to a reporting strategy that is undocumented and in disarray. End users will find themselves spending their valuable work hours tracking and generating reports instead of doing their jobs.

10.1 Types of information queries

Quests for financial information fall into several broad categories, depending on their nature and the reason behind the search. Each type fills a different reporting role by answering a different kind of question.

10.1.1 Operational reports

The first and most tedious types of reports are those that run regularly to support operational needs. Typically, these reports will run daily, weekly, monthly, quarterly, or annually to provide information to help end users verify the integrity of their departmental and organizational processes. Accounts payable check registers and vendor 1099 reports are examples of these types of reports. By and large, most of these reports are provided by PeopleSoft. Organizations might need to make minor modifications to chart field format and add fields pertinent to their business, but major modifications are probably not necessary. Reports for processes not supported by the base software will have to be designed and built during installation.

10.1.2 What is? reports

Another type of reporting question that PeopleSoft can answer is a simple "what is" question. What is the year-to-date activity for my department? What is the total dollar of 1099 activity for vendor XYZ? These types of questions are straightforward in that they generally return a single number to answer a specific question

10.1.3 Financial statements

All organizations must compile and publish periodic financial statements. Balance sheets and income statements typify this kind of report. These reports are most often produced using PC-based spreadsheet packages to take advantage of advanced formatting and charting capabilities. Often, report templates are used, and the difficult part of compiling these reports is generating the numbers to populate the spreadsheets.

10.1.4 Known search criteria

When end users know exactly the information they need, the only things left to do are to choose a reporting tool and design and generate the report. Suppose a division manager wants a listing of all departments in the division that are over budget on equipment purchases for the current fiscal year. That is a specific question, which easily translates into SQL statements and/or reporting logic. This type of report is most generally created on an ad hoc basis, because there are an unlimited number of questions that might be posed. Anticipating which reports will be needed at a specific time is nearly impossible.

10.1.5 Hunting trips

The most obscure reports are those where the search criteria are not known. From the outset, the end user is not sure exactly what he or she is looking for. It may be obvious that something is not quite right, but pinpointing the problem is not straight forward. The user may go back and forth between summary and detail information, drilling down to an appropriate level of detail in order to expose the problem. This type of report is extremely ad hoc and also iterative. It is a trek through a winding path of information, more so than a report creation.

The types of reports discussed above are not meant to be an exhaustive dissertation on the subject of financial reporting. They illustrate the vast differences among the various information requests posed to financial professionals. PeopleSoft obviously recognizes this and has set out to arm these professionals with the tools to effectively respond to all information requests. They have not always been successful. In the early days of PeopleSoft General Ledger, reporting was only moderately better than that of most traditional systems. Its nVision product was impressive and neoteric, but the remaining reporting tools required far too much programming expertise and did not free end users from the shackles of central information systems backlog. However, the reporting tools, since version 3.0 of PeopleSoft Financials, have been quite capable.

10.2 PeopleSoft reporting tools

10.2.1 Inquiry panels

PeopleSoft Financials application modules contain many specific query panels, which end users can use to obtain answers to common questions. In General Ledger, using the inquiry panels, an end user might query the ledger for period-to-date posted totals for a given account. In accounts

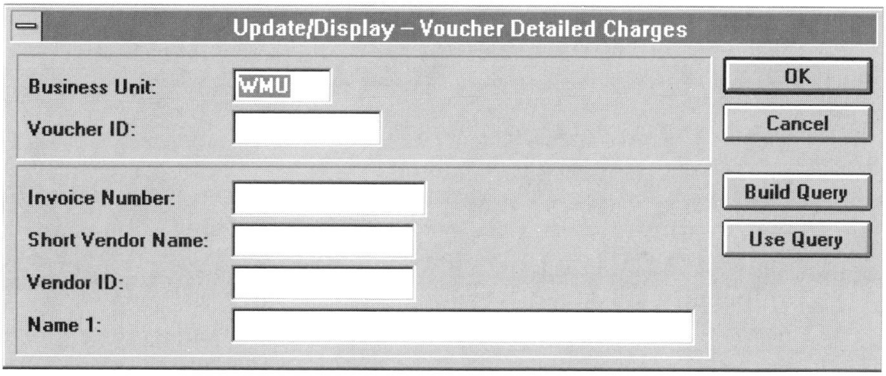

Figure 10.1 Inquiry panel

payable, the operators can query vouchers or payment based on a variety of parameters and views. (See Figure 10.1.)

Typically, a query panel is preceded by a search dialog box with a number of potential search keys by which the operator can request information. After entering some or all of the search criteria, the operator presses the OK button. PeopleSoft returns a panel full of details about the information being queried. Queries provide fast efficient answers to some specific but common financial questions. (See Figure 10.2.)

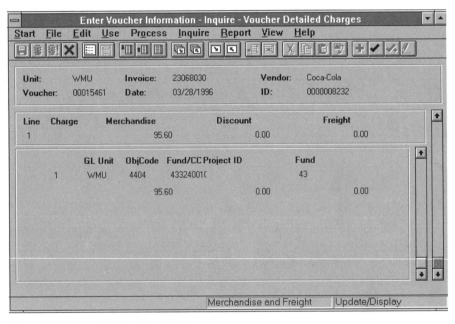

Figure 10.2 Expanded inquiry panel

10.2.2 PeopleSoft nVision

nVision is PeopleSoft's flagship and most impressive financial reporting tool. It brings together the power of the PeopleSoft Financials database and the flexibility and familiarity of Microsoft Excel. It is an Excel "add-in," manifested as a new menu option on the Excel menu bar. Using the new menu from within Excel, users create nVision layouts, which specify the contents and format for the report. nVision's capabilities and features include the following. (See Figure 10.3.)

- Designers can specify the contents and formatting as well as the scope of reports via dialog boxes from within Microsoft Excel.

- It summarizes information from chart fields, tree nodes, or levels, allowing reports to roll up ledger data in countless ways.

- Report layouts can generate multiple instances based upon the criteria of the scope—for example, a single layout could generate a report for every node in the division level of the department tree.

- Layouts pull information from PeopleSoft tables and nVision variables to populate row and column headings, allowing reports to change automatically over time as data change.

- Reports can generate summary information, but allow users to drill spreadsheet cells down to the underlying detail.

- Reports can access calendars, so they roll from period to period.

- Excel formulas, formatting, and charting options can be included directly in the layout for population and calculation by the report-generation process.

- nVision uses the PeopleSoft security schema to control access to the data.

- Reports can take advantage of Excel's built-in outline features to create reports that are easy to navigate.

- nVision includes two types of layouts. The *matrix layout* is the most complex and powerful. In a matrix layout, both row and column selection criteria are specified. Where these row and column criteria intersect, an SQL statement is created and executed against the database. Using matrix layouts, users can create complex reports, which are driven by detail chart field values, tree levels, or tree nodes. The only limitation of a matrix layout is that it can run against a tree. Since a tree can be created for almost any purpose, matrix layouts are practically limitless. Using the drill-down feature, it is even possible to query down to underlying journal entries. (See Table 10.1.)

The other type of layout is known as the *tabular layout*. It is more straight forward. Basically, a tabular report is made up of columns, which correspond to the fields selected in a database query. These data are retrieved by Excel for easy manipulation, but it is essentially no more than a query download directly into a spreadsheet.

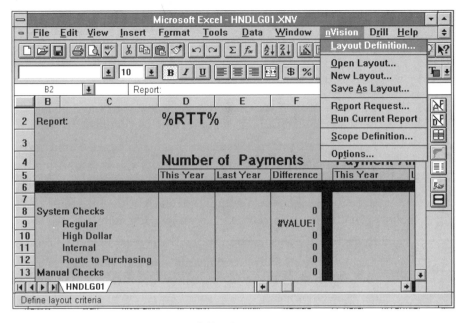

Figure 10.3 nVision menu in Microsoft Excel

Table 10.1 Steps to create an nVision matrix layout

Step	Description
Design the Layout	Create a new spreadsheet layout from within nVision, defining the structure of the report. This may include report headings and sheet sizes.
	Define the selection criteria for the entire spreadsheet. This may include such things as LEDGER, BUSINESS_UNIT, etc.
	Define the selection criteria for the rows and columns. These selections override those defined at the spreadsheet level.
	Enter report labels and formulas in the appropriate cells.
	Specify selection criteria for individual cells that are not based on the row and column selection already defined.
	Place nVision variables into the spreadsheet in the appropriate cells.
Determine the layout's scope	Scopes create multiple "instances," or copies, of the report, based on the criteria specified for the scope.
Define and Run the Report Request	Enter the descriptive information about this report, save it, and run the report.

nVision is an extremely complex but capable financial reporting tool. Few computer-savvy financial professionals will have difficulty grasping the basics of its functionality. However, the more advanced and advantageous features will require a significant investment in training, time, and effort to be effectively utilized.

10.2.3 Query

Traditional applications lacked a vehicle for end user data retrieval. Often, end user departments justified staffing a full-time programming position in order to generate on demand reports for their needs. Central information systems were loath to address these concerns, since they were responsible for transaction-based systems as opposed to information retrieval. This circumstance gave rise to myriad reporting tools, which sit on top of traditional software to provide access to end users. The reality of these solutions is that they still require substantial technical expertise to operate. The proliferation of relational database systems and SQL has given rise to a new breed of end user reporting tools. This new kind of query tool allows users to graphically choose tables and fields to generate an SQL statement to run against the database. People-Soft's Query is just such a tool. (See Figure 10.4.)

Query uses a tree structure of several available tables that users can point and click to select. Once a base table is selected, users are free to select fields, sort orders, look up table options, add expressions, build criteria logic, and join additional tables. Organizations have enough flexibility to match the expertise level of a particular end user with the functionality of Query. Experienced SQL programmers realize that the naive user, unchecked, can bring any RDBMS running on any hardware platform to its knees. It is essential that access to advanced functionality be limited to those who understand the complexities and implications of the SQL programming language. (See Table 10.2.)

Once a Query is created, it can be saved in one of two ways. Private queries are distinct to the operator who creates them. Only that operator will have access to view, edit, and run private queries. This should be used for queries that will never be shared. Public queries are ones that are available for all operators to view and execute. Access to public queries and database tables can be controlled by using query access groups. Access groups define access to "trees" of database tables. Each operator class has its own query security settings.

Table 10.2 Query user profile options

Query Use Options

  • Only allowed to run Queries

  • Allowed to create public Queries

  • Allowed to create workflow Queries

  • Set limit of maximum rows fetched

Advanced SQL Options

  • Allowed to use Distinct

  • Allowed to join any record

  • Allowed to use Subqueries or Exists

  • Allowed to use Union

  • Allowed to use Expressions

  • Set maximum number of Joins

  • Set maximum number of "In Tree" criteria

Query Output Options

  • User can output to a list box

  • User can output to a spreadsheet

  • User can output to Crystal Reports

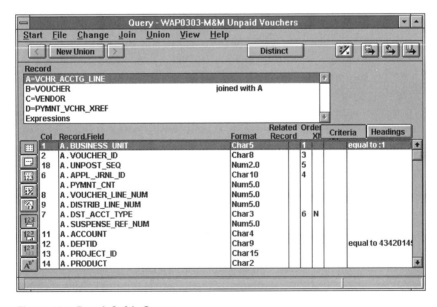

Figure 10.4 PeopleSoft's Query

Users have three options for the query output destination, which is selected at query execution time. The output can be sent to a Windows list box, so the user can briefly browse the information on the screen. The output can also be sent to a spreadsheet. Using the nVision interface, the query can ship data directly to a Microsoft Excel spreadsheet. This option will also work with Lotus 1-2-3. The final output destination option is to ship the query results to Crystal Reports. Crystal Reports is a Windows-based, point-and-click, drag-and-drop report design and generation tool. It is completely integrated with the Microsoft Windows printer drivers for excellent printing options.

10.2.4 Crystal Reports

PeopleSoft includes a version of Crystal Reports Professional. Crystal Reports is a WYSIWYG report designer, which is integrated with People-Soft's Query tool. End users and programmers define a query in People-Soft as the source record of a report in Crystal. Then, using point-and-click techniques, they can place database fields, text fields, formulas, and graphics on the page. Crystal takes full advantage of the Microsoft Windows printer drivers, so it has an infinite number of formatting options. PeopleSoft even uses Crystal Reports to generate laser checks, complete with MICR line and endorsing signatures.

10.2.5 SQR

SQR is really a programming language built around the SQL data retrieval language. It takes an experienced programmer to write an SQR program, and it is time consuming when compared with the other reporting tools. However, there are times when a complex report requires a significant amount of procedural programming logic. Query reports cannot contain complex processing logic, so, at times, SQR is the only option.

10.3 Matching reports to tools

An important component of an effective reporting environment is the selection of reporting tools for a given information requirement. Only within the context of the organization and the specific PeopleSoft installation can one accurately predict the best tool to answer a specific request for financial information. Some tools do, however, answer certain types of questions better than others. Table 10.3 demonstrates the complexity of tool-to-report matching.

Table 10.3 Tool/report matching

Type of Report	Inquiry	nVision	Query	Crystal Reports	SQR
Operational Reports	Poor	Poor	Fair	Good	Fair
What Is? Reports	Good	Poor	Good	Poor	Poor
Financial Statements	N/A	Good	Poor	Good	Fair
Known Search Criteria	Limited	Fair	Good	Fair	Poor
Hunting Trips	Limited	Good	Fair	Poor	Poor
Major Procedural Logic	N/A	Poor	N/A	Poor	Good

To reiterate, the strategy, of which this tool/report matching is a component, must be managed and logical. A programmer can develop any report using SQR, but to maintain that over time requires much more developer intervention than, for example, a Query or an nVision. A basic guideline is to develop the report using the least complex tool possible. In the matrix shown in Table 10.3, the tool selection should begin with the left-most "Inquiry"—and proceed sequentially to the most difficult tool—"SQR." In time, this decision will be intuitive for those who match the report with the appropriate tool.

10.4 Generating reports in PeopleSoft Financials

PeopleSoft's reporting tools are mostly integrated with its Process Scheduler batch program execution system. So, by and large, to generate a report, the operator simply accesses the panel containing the menu where the report option is found and selects the report from the menu. Typically, each report has an associated list of parameters, which are used as selection and format criteria. Once the operator enters the parameters, he or she then selects where the report should run and where the output should go and presses a special Run button on the PeopleSoft toolbar. To make the process even easier, developers can tailor the format of the parameter panels to include drop-down list boxes and other user-interface techniques to help guide the operator through the procedure and to minimize training and support requirements.

Two exceptions to this rule are SQR programs and Queries. SQR programs are usually the most complex of all. Tricky calculating programs, such as payment forecasting, require a significant amount of procedural logic, and PeopleSoft often opts to use SQR for them. This can be problematic for the novice PC operators, because SQR programs generate print files, which need to be sent manually to the printer. Even if creative network support specialists find a convenient method to print these reports, SQR programs are still less brainless than reports that take advantage of Crystal Reports. As for Queries, some of them are user friendly, because the operator simply opens and runs them. He or she has the option of sending the output to a list box, Crystal Reports, or nVision. However, if the operator is trying to create his or her own query, then it becomes a much more complicated task.

Another commonly overlooked issue is that of database understanding. A zealous and relatively well-off organization might put PeopleSoft workstations on the desks of all its employees and encourage them to query for information they can use to make better decisions. This seems ideal on the surface, but presents some challenges and risks. First, to train all end users to operate the reporting tools and how and when to apply the appropriate tool is a daunting task. The tools are difficult enough for programmers to learn, let alone the nontechnical and computer-shy end user. To compound the problem, even for the brightest of financial professionals, are the sheer size of the database, the number of tables, and their relationship to trees and each other. The risk faced by the organization is that an incorrect understanding of the tables will lead an end user to create an erroneous query, which retrieves incorrect results. That misinformation might be the basis for some business decision and has the potential for doing great harm. For this reason, the responsibility for accurate financial reporting must be formally and officially assigned to some group of individuals. By centrally managing report creation and requests for financial information, the organization can have some reasonable assurance that data used in decision making are accurate.

In general, organizations can establish operational reports that are effective and easy for end users to access and generate. Also, they can create financial statements and information queries requiring minimal operator intervention to fill most reporting needs. This cannot be a total solution, however, for answering all the requests for information required by changing business climates. Some balance among technical expertise, database knowledge, and PeopleSoft access must be achieved to provide the solution to the organization's reporting needs.

10.5 PeopleSoft deployment scope and reporting implications

The scope of PeopleSoft deployment has a major impact on precisely how the accounting department can distribute reports throughout the organization. If PeopleSoft Financials is widely installed in an organization, and departments can gain access to the tools to generate them, then reporting can be highly decentralized. The process still has to be managed and overseen, but at least the organization might move toward self-sufficient departmental reporting. If, on the other hand, PeopleSoft is not widely installed, but rather is more centrally operated and controlled, then deployment of the financial information is more troublesome. For this reason, the implementation team should consider the reporting needs and the expectations of executive management in this regard before making the final deployment scope decisions.

PeopleSoft Financials does provide a good deal of flexibility for distributing the reports produced in nVision and even in Crystal Reports. If the organization has a standard and managed local area network infrastructure established, then, by using nVision Scopes or Crystal Report distribution options, the reports can be distributed, electronically, to directory and file locations where each department can find them. This provides a means to create and distribute reports centrally throughout an organization. However, this only works for standard, predefined reports. So, monthly departmental operating reports can be sent to each department's network directory location. That does not help the manager who needs to ask a specific question not answered by that report. In most cases, there will be a gap between who actually has access to PeopleSoft and who needs to access information in PeopleSoft. The implementation team should seek to bridge this gap if at all possible.

One scenario is to create a central information center where department users and managers can call and submit financial questions. Answers can be transmitted electronically or printed, as in a traditional central information systems department. Another possibility is interactive voice response (IVR). Everyone is familiar with calling up the local bank and requesting detailed financial transaction information. IVR software running on top of PeopleSoft workstations might also provide some of the same capabilities. A more recent and better solution is to develop a corporate intranet based on World Wide Web technology and HTML. Using secure Web servers integrated with a relational database, all of the employees in an organization can access financial information complete with drill-down capabilities. They can also print the results to their local printer. This "Web" solution, while appealing to many, is a significant undertaking. It is not typically a good idea to open up your production database to endless queries by end users. It can degrade performance to the point where those relying on the PeopleSoft applications to do their jobs cannot complete them in time. The complexities and politics involved in such a solution dictate that it be a separate project, but it is one that is worth considering.

Financial reporting has been a major selling-point for PeopleSoft Financials since the days of General Ledger version 1.0. Its tight integration with Microsoft Excel, as well as the wealth of reporting tools, is indeed one of its greatest strengths. Developing a reporting environment within the organization is going to be an ongoing affair. Beginning with a baseline at production cutover, the information needs of the organization will drive the report development efforts. As long as those responsible for the financial information listen to the requests for information and seek to fill them in the most effective and efficient way possible, workers will have access to information that allows them to make more and better decisions in the battle for corporate survival.

chapter 11

Keys to success

So far, we have taken a look at some of the components involved in implementating PeopleSoft Financials and the challenges facing the project team. PeopleSoft, the corporation, is a successful and motivated application software vendor. It has experienced phenomenal growth through the first half of the 1990s. The software that PeopleSoft markets, specifically PeopleSoft Financials, is a manifestation of the PeopleSoft corporate culture. The Financials modules exemplify a new breed of software, which enables organizations using it to transform themselves into information- and knowledge-based organizations as opposed to the capital-based organizations common in the twentieth century. We have examined the technical complexity and discussed some of the functional issues that implementors face. The transition from a mainframe-centric application to a client/server application presents formidable obstacles, which organizations must overcome, and PeopleSoft is no exception. The consequences of a failed implementation can be devastating to the organization and the professionals on the project team. How can an implementation team guard against such catastrophe and ensure that its efforts end in success?

11.1 *What is success?*

To answer the question, "How can we be successful?" we must first define success. Many in the information systems business define project success as an engineer would: *meeting specification.* However, this answer is flawed from the beginning. To understand why, we need to highlight the differences between traditional engineering projects and software engineering projects.

11.1.1 *Traditional engineering projects*

Using the construction of a new house as an example, let's touch on the attributes of an engineering project. The project begins when someone requests a particular construction firm to build a new house. Generally, the customer already has a house plan picked out and delivers the blueprints to the construction manager to obtain an estimate. Using the blueprints as a guide, the manager prices all the materials needed and the labor required to complete the house as well as a time frame for completing it. He then presents the customer with a formal, written estimate stating precisely what the construction company will deliver and by when. Presumably, the customer signs an agreement with the firm, and the construction process begins. The project will have its ups and downs and its share of problems, but, in the end, the finished house will be the one that the customer requested—most likely within an acceptable tolerance of the target date as well. The only real way to botch this project is to drastically miss the target date, build the wrong house, or completely exceed the budget. The customer, however, is involved enough in the ongoing project to recognize when the project is going awry and to intercede to straighten its course.

11.1.2 *Software engineering projects*

Now, let's look at a typical software project. The customer approaches the information systems department and requests a new software system. The project team, by talking with the customer, tries to develop system specifications for the new application. When the requirements are gathered, the project manager creates a project plan, which discusses the specifications and puts forth a time frame for the project. After a time, the customer goes back to his or her department and the project team begins to construct the new application. During the construction process, the customer begins to add, change, and delete specifications. The developers add their own "bells and whistles" because "they're cool." Meanwhile, the business needs of the customer are steadily changing. Then, one day, probably long after the original target date, the project team finishes the installation of the new software. It is late, it is significantly different from the original specifications, and it may or may not actually meet the needs of the customer.

A major difference in the two projects is the definition of "success." In the construction project, clearly it is matching the customer's blueprints with reasonable financial and end-date tolerances. In the software project, success is measured more by the customer's satisfaction at the end of the project. To contrast the two: What if the construction firm had begun without blueprints? What if the customer said, "Build me a house on this lot and have it finished by a specific date?" Suppose the firm constructed a split-level house when the customer really wanted, but did not articulate, a ranch-style house? What if the construction project team picked out the carpet, paint and trim colors without consulting the customer? What would happen if, after the construction firm had finished framing the house, the customer asked for an additional bedroom or wanted the bathroom moved to the other side of the house after the plumbing was installed? These are outlandish hypotheses, but the analogy does apply to software projects. More often than not, these projects begin without a clear agreement of the specifications.

To clarify the assertion, success in a software project is completely subjective. Suppose two companies install PeopleSoft Financials. They both implement all available modules simultaneously, taking three years and 20 people to get them to production. One company might be delighted with these results, while the other is livid and considers punishing the project team. The key to understanding how this could be is to begin with the original expectations. If the expectation for Company A was for a three-year, "big-bang" implementation using 20 people, then its executives will be satisfied with the results. If Company B, however, expected some return on its investment within one year, then its executives will be sorely disappointed. Same project outcomes, different degrees of customer satisfaction. So, to state the definition: Software project success is the process of meeting organization and customer expectations within reasonable tolerances for time, money, and specifications. It is as simple as that. Define what will be done. Define who will do it, when it will be done, how it will be done, and possibly why it will be done—and obtain formal agreement for these "blueprints" between the project team, the customers, and executive management before the project is started. By obtaining this agreement, the project team puts the responsibility for the project's *goals* where it belongs: on executive management. Once that is done, the project team can set about following the project plan until it is complete. If it is successful at completing the tasks per specification and generally on time, then the results should match the original expecations. Executive management and customers are happy and the project is perceived to be a success.

The project team that listens to its customers; develops *their* specifications (not those of the team); sets the expectations by communicating the project plan and the specifications with the customers and executive management; carries out the plan accordingly; and produces a finished product, which very nearly meets the expectations, will be perceived as a successful project team. Those who do not do these things, will be perceived as unsuccessful, affecting future assignments, financial rewards, and professional futures. This is why project leadership is so critical and why behavioral issues outweigh technical ones.

11.2 Implementation checklist

So, how does the PeopleSoft Financials implementation team guarantee success? Clearly, it is critical to meet with executive management in the beginning and discuss their expectations for the new software. The project leader must present the various strategies to them, forcing them to choose the one that most clearly meets their requirements. Several options, from implementing one module at a time—in succession, using a team of only four members—to implementing all financial modules simultaneously, using a team of 20, must be presented as valid alternatives. The executives can set the agenda for the entire project, which is their responsibility anyway. The project leader must also consistently and effectively communicate the project plan at each and every stage. It will not be clear, for example, how much time will be involved in software customizations until *after* the prototyping sessions are finished, but when it is clear, then he or she should update the plan and communicate the assumptions, assertions, strategies, specifications, and time frames to executive management. By keeping their expectations in line with reality, the project leader is ensuring that the implementation will be successful.

Aside from that single issue, however, this entire book has been dedicated to arming the project team with the tools necessary to "do People-Soft right." The following list summarizes the major issues, challenges, and responsibilities that make up a successful implementation. By ensuring that each item is properly addressed within the context of the specific organization, the project leader will minimize the chance of failure and potentially increase the return on investment of the PeopleSoft Financials software acquisition.

- PeopleSoft Financials is properly suited for the organization
- Proper training
  - Technical skills
  - Database administration skills
  - Networking expertise
  - Business acumen of the functional areas
  - PeopleSoft expertise and/or experience
  - Executive briefings
- Effective project team
  - Skilled, proven project leader
  - Line managers are included
  - Executive sponsor is included
  - Team skills match the project's goals
- The project plan
  - Identify the scope of software deployment
    - Centralized versus decentralized
    - How far out in the organization will the software extend and why?
  - Phase the implementation
    - If not, executive management is aware of the extended time frame
  - Estimate only what you know

- Keep each task under 80 hours
- Prioritize features and requirements
  - Low-priority features can be eliminated to meet the deadline
- Assess the project's risks and share them with executive management
- Establish a change budget to avoid "scope creep"
- Consistently communicate the project plan
  - Better too much to too many than too little to too few
- Establish effective status reporting
- Installation
  - Be certain the technology is maintainable
    - Establish and document standards
  - Install high-end workstations
  - Address remote-access issues if necessary
- Implementation options
  - Model the current business processes
  - Consider business process reengineering
    - PeopleSoft is an excellent opportunity for it
    - Ask for input from other departments
    - Market the benefits
  - Establish effective and rational chart fields
  - Conduct product "Prototyping" sessions
    - To help reengineer business processes
    - To make implementation decisions
    - To establish security profiles
    - To identify customizations
- PeopleSoft Financials customizations
  - Understand the upgrade architecture
  - Don't if you can help it
  - Extend the system
    - Isolate your modifications from PeopleSoft objects and processes

- Avoid modifying the batch COBOL programs
- Document all modifications for reference during upgrades
- Interfaces to other systems
  - Identify all of them
- Data conversion
  - Define the conversion scope
  - Thoroughly map the data from old to new
  - Study the PeopleSoft data models to understand the applications
  - Use the best-fit tool for the job
  - Leverage existing knowledge of legacy systems
- Testing
  - Unit test customizations
  - Perform complete integration testing
  - Perform stress testing
    - To ensure the application will support the transaction and offline processing loads
- Cutover to production
  - Make implementation Team available to fight fires
  - Make sure the team agrees on the "go-live" date
  - Set the expectations for that time period
    - There will be problems for a short while
- Performance tuning
  - Set performance expectations up front
  - Record benchmark timings of basic functions
  - Listen to the end users
    - They will highlight performance problems
- Financial reporting strategy
  - Manage the reporting
  - Use the appropriate tool
  - Consider the scope of deployment when formulating the reporting strategy

bibliography

Implementing PeopleSoft Applications, PeopleSoft, Inc., 1995

PeopleSoft Financial Application User Guides, PeopleSoft, Inc., 1995

PeopleSoft PeopleTools User Guide, PeopleSoft, Inc., 1995

Byham, William C. with Cox Jeff, *Zapp! The Lightning of Empowerment,* Ballentine Books, 1988

"Fortune's 25 Coolest Companies," *Fortune* Magazine, July 10, 1995

Horniman, Alexander, "Lessons from High Performance Teams," A Presentation at *Project Leadership Conference,* June 1995.

PeopleSoft Hardware and Software Requirements, PeopleSoft, Inc., 1995

Bancroft, Nancy H., *Implementing SAP R/3,* Manning Publications, 1996

The Keane Approach to Project Management, Keane, Inc., 1995

Comaford, Christine, "To Customize or Not to Customize," *PC Week,* March 1995

Southwick, Karen, "Going for the Jugular," *Upside,* online, November 1995

glossary

In a PeopleSoft project, it is important that those involved speak a common language. While the specific terminology applying to each functional module is beyond the scope of this book and is, perhaps, a book in itself, the common terms found in the PeopleSoft applications and the context of the implementation project are as follows.

Access ID   Peoplesoft's Access ID is the database logon ID, which the PeopleSoft applications use when connected to the database. It is different from the User ID, which is the one that end users log on with. PeopleSoft, in a background operation, signs the user off and back on using the Access ID. This greatly simplifies the task of establishing security profiles for the underlying database.

Account Manager   The account manager is the main point of contact between the customer and PeopleSoft. He or she is responsible for helping to ensure successful implementations. This is not the sales representative with whom an organization negotiated.

Accounts Payable   Accounts Payable is a PeopleSoft module used to manage an organization's accounts payable department. It includes support for vendors, 1099 processing, and invoice entry.

Accounts Receivable   Accounts Receivable is a PeopleSoft module used to manage an organization's accounts receivable department.

Actions	A PeopleSoft Action is the vehicle by which a user communicates to the applications whether to Update, Display, or Correct rows in a table. Update/Display only retrieves current and future rows, while Update/Display All retrieves history rows as well. Correction allows the user to make changes to existing records rather than adding another effective-dated record.
API	API stands for Application Programming Interface. It is a generic term used to identify a standard method for communicating with an application. Microsoft's OLE is an example of an API. PeopleTools includes APIs for functions such as Workflow and user-defined C routines.
Application Data Tables	Application data tables are the tables of a PeopleSoft database, which holds the organizations information. Information such as general ledger journal entries, chart of account values, vendors, and fixed asset information are stored in data tables.
Application Engine	The PeopleSoft Application Engine is a People-Tools tool, which allows developers to create set-driven, offline processes or programs. It can perform functions such as SQL statements and it can call COBOL subprograms, too. Some of PeopleSoft's own offline programs are written using the Application Engine.
Application Upgrade	An Application Upgrade is the process of updating the functional part of the PeopleSoft application. This generally results in additional functionality for the end user.
Asset Management	Asset Management is a PeopleSoft module for managing an organization's fixed assets inventory.
Benchmark	A benchmark is a performance target established during performance testing. Benchmarks

are recorded to identify normal processing speed for certain transactions and to develop a range that is "normal." Benchmarks can be used to confirm performance problems that develop and can serve as input to performance-tuning functions.

Billing

Billing is a PeopleSoft module for compiling bills and printing invoices including discounts, surcharges, and taxes.

Business Process

A business process is a procedure that an organization defines as standard operating procedure. Generally, it has inputs, value-added transformation, and outputs.

Business Process Reengineering

Business Process Reengineering, or BPR, is the task of analyzing an organization's business processes in light of existing business conditions and economic pressures, with the goal of streamlining them and attaining new levels of efficiency.

Business Rule

Business rules are established operating procedures identified as appropriate and necessary for the effective operation of the organization. A business rule might be: All 1099 vendors must have a tax-ID before they will be issued a check. Business rules are often changed when implementing PeopleSoft Financials.

Business Unit

Business unit is a fundamental, high-level entity of the PeopleSoft Financials data model. It means different things to different modules; thus it is a source of confusion. PeopleSoft defines Business Unit to be: A corporation or a subset of a corporation that is independent with regard to one or more accounting functions. PeopleSoft General Ledger business units typically comprise individual entities for tax-accounting purposes. PeopleSoft Project Costing business units represent operational structures, but not necessarily independent financial units. PeopleSoft Payables business units are either Vouching (have payables accrued to them) or Charge to (have voucher expense distributions charged to them) and pass journals to general ledger units. People-Soft Purchasing business units share vendor, purchase order, and receiving information with PeopleSoft Payables units in the same SetID. A PeopleSoft Inventory business unit is a storage facility that maintains its own set of inventory transactions, as well as its own definitions and guidelines.

Change Budget

A project Change Budget is a mechanism for managing the scope inflation of a software project. By allowing a predetermined amount of additional functionality and/or time to be "purchased," it gives the project team flexibility and gives management some level of control over that flexibility.

Chart Field

Chart fields are the fundamental accounting entities of an organization's financial system. For the most part, chart fields support strategic planning in that they allow for the effective analysis of financial data by some or all of the chart fields at any given time.

Client / Server

Client/server is the term assigned to software that is comprised of multiple tiers. In its simplest terms, one process, the client, requests data and/or work from another process, the server. PeopleSoft is a client/server software application.

COBOL

COBOL, or COmmon, Business Oriented Language, is a 3GL programming language commonly used for business applications. It continues to dominate the industry in terms of lines of code running in production. It has fallen out of favor by "fashionable" developers, but remains an appropriate language in which to develop offline applications. PeopleSoft uses COBOL for its most critical offline processes such as General Ledger posting.

Crystal Reports

Crystal Reports is a Windows-based, WYSI-WYG report development package from Seagate Software. PeopleSoft packages Crystal Reports with its software as one of its primary reporting methods.

Customizations

Customizations are changes made to the PeopleSoft applications by the organization. While they should be minimized, some will be inevitably necessary because of business requirements.

Data Conversion

Data conversion is the process of extracting information from old files, manipulating it, and loading it into PeopleSoft application tables.

Data Designer

Data Designer is the foundational tool in the PeopleTools development suite. With it, developers define relational tables and views, which are used throughout their applications. It is also used for database administration and maintenance tasks.

Data Mapping

Data mapping is the process in the data conversion phase of an implementation that defines how an organization's existing financial data maps to the fields and records in the PeopleSoft database. It is an intricate process, which requires both end users and programmers to work together.

Data Model

The data model is the logical structure of the PeopleSoft application database. It manifests itself as tables in the relational database system. PeopleSoft delivers a graphical representation of its data models with the software, which developers and end users can use to gain an understanding of the software's scope and process flow.

Data Mover	Data Mover is a PeopleTools application, which assists in data management. It allows developers and database administrators to load and unload data to and from PeopleSoft databases. It uses a device-independent format, which allows databases to be copied to and from different relational database systems such as ORACLE and DB2.
Database	A database is a collection of entities and relationships that are implemented as tables filled with rows of data. A PeopleSoft database consists of the application data tables, which store the organization's information, and PeopleTools tables, which store the applications' programs.
Database Administration	The process of monitoring and adjusting a working database is known as database administration. This is usually a term referring to the "care and feeding" of a relational database. Typically, a database requires a good deal of performance tuning, data reorganization, backup, and system parameter manipulation as the database grows over time. Failure to provide proper administration can lead to disaster.
Database Server	This is a term usually referring to the physical computer on which the relational database management system runs—for example, if ORACLE runs on an RS/6000, which holds all of the application's data, then the RS/6000 would be referred to as a database server.
DDL	DDL is the acronym for Data Definition Language. This is the portion of the structured query language database programming language that defines the actual structure of the database.

Using DDL, database administrators create tables, drop tables, and manipulate indexes.

Deployment

Deployment is the process of rolling out software to end users. Deployment is an often-overlooked task, which can be extremely problematic. Understanding the nature and scope of deployment from the outset of the project is critical to properly define the project.

Detail Panels

Detail panels are panels that are used during the SEARCH PANEL process to verify that an end user is selecting the appropriate record. Usually, a detail panel is defined for each panel group, which allows the end users to examine individual records efficiently before entering Update mode.

DML

Data Manipulation Language (DML) is the portion of the structure query language database programming language that changes data. INSERT, UPDATE, and DELETE statements are examples of DML statements. DML is the only way to change data in a relational database. PeopleTools uses DML behind the scenes to change data in the database tables.

Effective Date

This is a method of dating information in PeopleSoft applications. End users can predate information to add historical data or postdate information to enter it before it actually goes into effect.

Executive Sponsor

This is the individual in an organization who has the political clout to undertake the PeopleSoft implementation project. That person is not typically involved in the project operation day-to-day, but must be available for resource allocation and must be kept informed of project progress.

File Server

File server is a network computer, which multiple users connect to in order to access and share files and programs and share printers. It can be thought of as an electronic filing cabinet for all types of information. It is different from a database server, which houses the relational database for the PeopleSoft applications.

Financial Statements

These are financial reports, which are massaged and published. They reflect an organization's performance. Typically these are some of the most demanding reports to compile and often are in spreadsheet form. PeopleSoft uses nVision to prepare financial statements.

General Ledger

This is an integrated financial database with general ledger accounting, budgeting, financial analysis, and reporting features.

Help Designer

Help Designer is a PeopleTools application that allows developers and end users to customize online help, so that it reflects the operation of a given organization. Effective use of Help Designer can lead to reduced support requirements.

Hotline

The customer support telephone network is known as the hotline C. When PeopleSoft customers have problems with the software, they call the hotline for solutions.

HTML

HTML is the acronym for HyperText Markup Language. It is the standard protocol for creating World-Wide-Web documents on the Internet.

Implementation Partner

This is a third-party firm that collaborates with PeopleSoft customers to help them through a successful implementation.

Import Manager

This is a PeopleTools application which allows programmers to load sequential files into PeopleSoft database tables. Typically, it is used for data conversion. The major advantage of Import Manager is that it executes certain types of PeopleCode that enforce online edit rules.

Integration Testing

Integration testing is a type of application software testing that involves testing the entire system from a macro level. It measures how the software actually interoperates within itself. It is typically the last testing completed before parallel testing.

Interface

A process that moves data from one system to another is known as an interface. General Ledger, for example, has an interface that allows external systems to load journal entries into the system. Interfaces are typically defined and rigid. They are the vehicle whereby information travels between software applications. Other examples of interfaces are between General Ledger and Payroll or other line of business applications.

Internet

The conceptual network that ties together countless subnetworks into one large logical network is known as the Internet. It relies on the TCP/IP network communication protocol. Recently, the Internet has grown in size with the rising popularity of the World Wide Web.

Intranet

This is a mini Internet within a single organization or a few organizations. In reality, it involves a TCP/IP network within an organization that houses one or more World Wide Web servers to manage, collect, or distribute information or products.

Inventory

This is a PeopleSoft application for replenishment, order fulfillment, and management of inventory levels and warehouse space.

LAN

LAN is the acronym for Local Area Network. It is a small network, which ties together many users and allows them to share print services, file services, and perhaps database services.

Legacy Programmer

A legacy programmer is a programmer who has spent years programming in third-generation languages such as COBOL. Often, they are the most knowledgeable programmers, but lack expertise in the new methods of programming, such as graphical user interface, event-driven programming, and relational databases. They can be an invaluable tool in the implementation, if they are trained and used appropriately. Organizations sometimes make the mistake of labeling them as less capable and therefore miss opportunities that would benefit both the project team and the legacy programmers.

Line of Business Application

This is an application specific to a vertical industry—for example, in the higher-education market, a Student Information System is a line of business application. It would not be found in a different market such as automobile manufacturing.

Mass Change

A PeopleTools application, Mass Change is a set-processing tool which manipulates a set of rows in the database corresponding to one or more related tables. It can also be used to archive data, copy rows of data from one table to another, and perform common transactions not supported using the PeopleSoft panels.

Menu Designer

Menu Designer is used to organize PeopleSoft panels produced using Panel Designer into logical groups for access by end users.

Methodology

This is a formal process for accomplishing a task. Often it is associated with methods of software development or project structure.

Microsoft Windows

Microsoft Windows is a task-switching operating environment by Microsoft. It originated in the late 1980s and came to prominence in the early 1990s. It is currently available in multiple forms—the most common being Windows

	3.1, Windows 95, and Windows NT. PeopleSoft requires Windows on the users' workstations.
nVision	PeopleSoft's flagship and most impressive financial reporting tool is known as nVision. It brings together the power of the PeopleSoft Financials database and the flexibility and familiarity of Microsoft Excel. It is an Excel "add-in" manifested as a new menu option on the Excel menu bar.
Object Security	This is security tool used to control access to application development objects. With it, organizations can restrict which employees can modify particular portions of the software including Panels, Records, Trees, and so forth.
Operational Reports	Reports that support the day-to-day operations of a department or organization are called operational reports. An accounts payable operational report might be, for example, a daily check register. Often these reports can be online, saving printer wear and paper.
Operator Class	An operator class is a set security access, which can be assigned to multiple individuals. In theory, it groups common access, so it can be more easily maintained. In practice, People-Soft version 5 does not support multiple classes per user, as nuances between users require too many classes to be used efficiently.
Operator Security	This is a PeopleTools application for defining and maintaining user access to PeopleSoft applications such as General Ledger and Accounts Payable.
Panel Designer	A PeopleTools application for creating screens, forms, or panels. It is a visual development tool much like Visual BASIC, where programmers drag fields and controls onto forms and tie them to database fields in the database.

Panel Group	This is a group of panels that share the same search record. They are used to implement a transaction that spans more than one panel. Panel groups are one of PeopleSoft's most powerful features in that they allow multilevel and multipanel transactions, which can span many database tables.
Panels	The basic user-interaction entity of a People-Soft application is a panel. Panels are really screens with which end users interact.
Parallel Testing	Parallel testing is a type of testing that is done to compare results of an old system with those of a new one. It is a vehicle for ensuring that the business needs of the organization are being met and that the new applications work before unplugging the legacy system.
People Dollars	People Dollars are pretend money issued to PeopleSoft customers for the express purpose of voting for enhancements to be included in the next release. Typically, each organization gets $100 for each module. They can apply that $100, in any ratio, to identified or other enhancements.
PeopleCode	The programming language used to add procedural logic to online PeopleSoft applications is known as PeopleCode. It is tied to a field on a record. PeopleCode follows a field/record across all panels in the application.
PeopleTools	This is a generic term, which refers to the collection of online software development tools and offline data management tools used to build applications in the PeopleSoft product environment. These tools include Data Designer, Panel Designer, Menu Designer, Operator Security, Object Security, Workflow, Application Engine, Mass Change, Query, nVision, Data Mover, and Import Manager.

Other tools, such as SQR, COBOL, and Crystal Reports, are also included in the development suite, but are generally not referred to as PeopleTools.

PeopleTool Tables	These are tables in the relational database that actually hold the components of the application. They hold, for example, the definitions of all records, panels, and menus for an application, but they do not hold the organizational data, such as journal entries and ledger balances.
PeopleTools Upgrade	This is an upgrade enhancing the functionality of PeopleTools. There is no change to an application's functionality. Usually, this upgrade is done in conjunction with application upgrades when PeopleSoft releases a new version.
Performance Testing	Performance testing measures the speed with which the application runs. It is important, because some processes in PeopleSoft can be time-consuming, and organizations often have time constraints. Without this type of testing, the project team risks moving something to production that cannot logistically run.
Performance Tuning	The process of manipulating database settings and programs to attain higher levels of performance is known as performance tuning. It can involve programmers, database administrators, end users, and network specialists in the PeopleSoft environment.
Policies	Stated procedures to be adhered to by an organization are known as policies. These should be targets for review during business process reengineering efforts.
Process Scheduler	Process Scheduler is a job automation, PeopleTools application allowing for the scheduling, tracking, and running of offline or batch programs. These include items such as journal

posting and check generation as well as reports.

Production   Production refers to the working version of software on which an organization relies to complete its business functions. Typically, organizations have such versions as test, production, demo, training, and others.

Production Cutover   This is the act of moving software from test or quality assurance to production status. It is usually a stressful and risky process, but is a point of success for a project team.

Project Costing   Project Costing is an integrated financial database combined with project tracking, budgeting, analysis, and reporting tools.

Project Leader   The member of a project team who is responsible for the success or failure of the project is the project leader. It is a demanding role, which involves more behavioral issues than traditional management and scheduling functions. It is the most critical position of the team.

Project Plan   The project plan includes the schedule, methodology, and resources assigned and defined for a given project.

Prototype   This is the process of reviewing PeopleSoft applications and modifying or discussing modifications and how they will affect the organization and the software. It is typically the vehicle whereby customizations are identified and parameters are established for setting up PeopleSoft Financials applications.

Purchasing   Purchasing is a PeopleSoft application for requisitioning, purchasing, and receiving raw materials, supplies, services, products, and assets.

Query	Query is a PeopleTools application for graphically creating information lookup profiles from a PeopleSoft application. Using Query, end users create queries on an ad hoc basis.
Rapid Application Development	This is the process of rapidly developing programs and systems using prototyping as a methodology.
Relational Database	Relational databases are databases built on the mathematical model of data structures developed by E. F. Codd. Generally, they run on a separate server CPU and service SQL requests for data. PeopleSoft runs only on relational databases.
Remote Access	This is a vehicle enabling remote sites to access a PeopleSoft application. It is a technically tricky endeavor to establish a remote access system, but is a popular means for distributing the PeopleSoft applications for organizations with multiple locations.
Risk Assessment	The process of identifying the likely factors that will keep a development project from completion is known as risk assessment. All projects should have a risk assessment completed in their early stages.
Scope Creep	This term refers to the tendency for software projects to continually add features and functions to the application. It is a major reason why projects are consistently late and over-budget.
Search Records	These are records in PeopleSoft applications used to retrieve rows from the database to be updated from a panel.
Spreadsheet	A spreadsheet is a financial information productivity tool used by accountants to reflect financial numbers and to analyze financial

information. PeopleSoft integrates with Microsoft Excel using nVision.

SQL   Structured Query Language (SQL) is a standard database programming language used to retrieve and manage data in relational database management systems. Using SQL, users can request operations of a database with an English-like syntax, significantly reducing the amount of manual programming required and easing information retrieval.

SQR   SQR is the acronym for Structured Query Reporting by Miti. It is an SQL-based programming language, which PeopleSoft uses to run some of its most sophisticated offline processes and reports. It is similar in some ways to COBOL and is easy for legacy programmers to learn.

Stress Testing   The process of testing software's capability to handle high transaction loads is known as stress testing.

Swap Files   Swap files are files on the local drive of a workstation that speed the performance of PeopleSoft applications. They contain information about panels, records, and PeopleCode programs. Swap files are automatically updated when one of these is changed by a programmer.

System Catalog Tables   These are tables in a relational database that the database itself uses to keep track of records, fields, indexes, views, security, and so forth.

TableSet   This is a complete set of tables defining accounting structure and rules. These tables control entry types and reason codes, payment terms, statement formats, operator parameters, distribution codes, and so forth. TableSets enable organizations to define multiple accounting structures, so that multiple companies or operating entities can work with the calendars, accounts, and so forth reflecting the way each does business.

Training Units   These are units charged to organizations for using training from PeopleSoft. Each PeopleSoft course costs a specific number of training units, which can be purchased from PeopleSoft at a negotiated price.

Tree   The graphical hierarchy in PeopleSoft systems displaying the relationship between all accounting units (e.g., corporate divisions, projects, reporting groups, and account numbers) and determining roll-up hierarchies.

Tree Manager   The PeopleTools application used to create and maintain PeopleSoft trees is the Tree Manager.

Unit Testing   Unit testing is a type of testing, used by programmers, to ensure that individual pieces of program code function as expected.

Upgrade Manager   This is the PeopleTools application used to upgrade PeopleSoft modules with a new release and to apply customizations to an already in-production database.

User ID   The user ID is used by the end user to log into the PeopleSoft application.

WAN   WAN is the acronym for Wide Area Network. It refers to a network consisting of two or more connected, local area networks. WANs are often used by organizations that have remote locations, such as banks.

Workflow   This is a PeopleTools application used to define roles, responsibilities, and processes that automate the flow of work and/or information within an organization.

Workstation   Workstations are the end users' computers.
                                They are typically Intel-based personal com-
                                puters running one of the Microsoft Windows
                                operating systems.

index